"Joseph Thoburn was both a physician and a warrior. His martial skills caused him to stand out among his peers in Maj. Gen. Philip H. Sheridan's Army of the Shenandoah. The Scotch-Irish immigrant became an outstanding brigade and division commander who left his mark on the numerous battlefields of the 1864 Shenandoah Valley Campaign. His diary provides keen insight into the workings of Thoburn's mind and likewise provides keen insight into the physician-turned-warrior's battlefield exploits. Scott Patchan, the dean of 1864 Valley Campaign historians, has done a fine job of editing Thoburn's diary and getting it ready for publication. This diary will become an important resource for any historian seeking to document the fighting that occurred in the Shenandoah Valley in 1864 and will be an excellent source for those who enjoy reading primary sources."

- **Eric J. Wittenberg,** award-winning author

"This is a gem of a journal – particularly because it comes from the hand of a brigade and division commander, perhaps one of the Civil War's most underappreciated Union martyrs. Colonel Joseph Thoburn's insights and details provide abundant grist for understanding and appreciating the first three months of the 1864 Shenandoah Valley Campaign. Scott Patchan's expertise as the leading authority of the campaign enhances this rich account with adept annotations as well as valuable bookends to the journal, including Thoburn's life and career before his first journal entry and his heroic performances and untimely death after his final one. After completing this enjoyable read, one cannot escape the mix of hope and regret that appear from the realization that Thoburn's earlier journals of the War may still exist but have yet to be discovered."

- **Gary Ecelbarger,** a leading authority on the 1862 Shenandoah Valley Campaign

Worthy of a Higher Rank

The 1864 Shenandoah Valley Campaign Journal

of

Colonel Joseph Thoburn, Commander

First Infantry Division, Army of West Virginia

by Scott C. Patchan

35th Star Publishing
Charleston, West Virginia
www.35thstar.com

Copyright. © 2021 by Scott C. Patchan.
All Rights Reserved.
Printed in the United States of America.

No part of this publication may be reproduced, distributed or transmitted in any form or by any means, including photocopying, recording, or other electronic or mechanical methods, without the prior written permission of the publisher, except in the case of brief quotations embodied in critical reviews and certain other noncommercial uses permitted by copyright law.

ISBN-13: 978-1-7350739-8-9
ISBN-10: 1-7350739-8-9
Library of Congress Control Number: 2021942646

35th Star Publishing
Charleston, West Virginia
www.35thstar.com

On the cover: Images of Colonel Joseph Thoburn, flag, and his sword are from the Suzanne Pezick Collection.

Cover design by Studio 6 Sense - www.studio6sense.com

Publisher's Cataloging-in-Publication Data
Names: Patchan, Scott C., author.
Title: Worthy of a Higher Rank: The 1864 Shenandoah Valley Campaign Journal of Colonel Joseph Thoburn, Commander, First Infantry Division, Army of West Virginia / Scott C. Patchan
Description: First edition. | Charleston, West Virginia : 35th Star Publishing, 2021. | Includes bibliographical references and index.
Identifiers: ISBN 978-1-7350739-9-6.
Subjects: BISAC: HISTORY / United States / CivilWar Period (1850-1877) | NONFICTION / Biography & Autobiography

To the memory of my father, Raymond J. Patchan

Yours truly
J. Thoburn

Table of Contents

Acknowledgments xv
Introduction - Colonel Thoburn and the Valley of Humiliation 1
Foreword - by Bishop James M. Thoburn 19

1 - The New Market Campaign 21

2 - The Battle of Piedmont and Capture of Staunton 33

3 - Hunter's Raid on Lynchburg 45

4 - Back to the Valley: Chasing Jubal Early's Raiders 57

5 - The Second Battle of Kernstown and Another Retreat 71

6 - A Change of Command 79

Prologue - Sheridan's Valley Campaign 89

Appendix A - Letters from the 1st West Virginia Infantry and Colonel Joseph Thoburn 119

Appendix B - Colonel Thoburn's Report on the Battle of Piedmont 127

Appendix C - Accounts of Thoburn's Death 131

Bibiography 135
Notes 137
Index 153
About the Author 163

Illustrations

Col. Joseph Thoburn   ix
Col. Thoburn's sword and scabbard   2
Thoburn's headquarters flag   3
Kate Ann Mitchell Thoburn   6
Mrs. Thoburn, Ann Lyle, and Joseph Thoburn, 1856   6
Mrs. Thoburn holding Anna Lyle, 1856   6
Thoburn children   7
Col. Benjamin F. Kelley   9
Thoburn's photo wallet   10
Maj. Gen. John Pope   16
Bishop James M. Thoburn   19
Thoburn's diary and excerpt   22
Thomas C. Thoburn   23
Captain John Carlin   27
Map: Battle of New Market   28
Maj. Gen. Franz Sigel   31
Map: Battle of Piedmont   40
View of Piedmont Battlefield   41
View of Piedmont Battlefield   43
Corporal Joseph Halstead   44
Maj. Gen. David Hunter   46
Col. George D. Wells   51
Map: Shenandoah Valley Campaign of 1864   59
Map: Battle of Cool Spring   62
Cool Spring Battlefield   64
Lt. James H. Rider   66
Col. Daniel Frost   69
Brevet Maj. Gen. George Crook   73
Map: Second Battle of Kernstown   74
Col. William B. Curtis   78
Captain Robert S. Gardner   81
Col. Jacob M. Campbell   85

Illustrations (Cont.)

Maj. Gen. Philip H. Sheridan   87
Captain George Macomber   94
Col. Isaac H. Duval   98
James E. Taylor sketch: Crook's Headquarters   104
James E. Taylor sketch: Foul Murder of Col. Thoburn   109
Frederick County home where Thoburn died   112
Telegraph regarding death of Thoburn   113
Captain Philip G. Bier   114
Daily Intelligencer headlines concerning funeral of Thoburn   115
Grave of Col. Thoburn   116

Acknowledgments

It is only through the assistance of many individuals that publication of this book was made possible. Their efforts are greatly appreciated and acknowledged henceforth. Back in the early 1990's while I was researching for my first book on the Battle of Piedmont, Chuck Critchfield of Clarksburg, West Virginia, informed me of the original typescript published by Col. Thoburn's grandson in 1914 and provided me with a copy that proved invaluable for several book projects. Without him, this project would never have occurred. Suzanne Pezick of Greensboro, North Carolina, Thoburn's great-great granddaughter provided photographs, pre-war journals and made his sword and flag from his funeral available for photographing, making the drive from her home in North Carolina to Winchester, Virginia. She is also in possession of the original, which contains a few key passages revealing Thoburn's opinions on his commanders that were omitted from the original typescript publication. Her enthusiasm for this project helped me get through some of the duller points of production and inspired me to see it through to publication.

Rick Wolfe of Bridgeport, West Virginia, and Nicholas Picerno of Bridgewater, Virginia, shared photographs from their collections for use in this book. Terry Lowry of Charleston, West Virginia, shared copies of Thoburn's report on the battle of Piedmont from the West Virginia State Archives. Dana McBean of Greenville, South Carolina, and

Ann Sindelar of the Western Reserve Historical Society assisted with the *James Taylor Sketchbook*. Gary Ecelbarger of Annandale, Virginia, shared sources on the 1862 Valley Campaign, and Margaret Brennan of Wheeling, West Virginia, provided copies of articles from the Wheeling Daily Intelligencer related to Thoburn's activities outside of the Valley as well as other local history information. Margaret also took time to give me a tour of Thoburn and Civil War related sites in Wheeling. Author Charles R. Knight and Savas Beatie Publishing provided the map of the Battle of New Market. Much appreciation is also extended to Mary Thoburn of Medina, Ohio, who kindly furnished me with a copy of Major Thomas Thoburn's journal, which included several letters written by his brother Joseph.

Finally, I extend hearty thanks to Steve Cunningham of 35th Star Publishing in Charleston, West Virginia, for enthusiastically taking on this project and patiently working with me as we went through the process.

Introduction

Colonel Thoburn and the Valley of Humiliation

The aromatic smoke emanating from pipes and cigars wafted through the air of the Opera House in Wheeling, West Virginia. A large crowd of U. S. Army veterans gathered in reunion nearly twenty years after the Civil War had ended. These men, formerly young, hardy soldiers who had fought in the ranks of the 1st West Virginia Infantry during that bloody conflict, reunited with comrades, many of whom they had not seen since the war ended. "Lusty cheering, [and] hearty greetings" dominated the scene along with other expressions of the "fellowship that during the dark days of war bound men closer together than brothers." While the reunion brought forth the manly clasping of hands and jovial cheering, tears of grief elicited by memories of soldiers' shared trials dampened the cheeks of many a veteran as they embraced former comrades in arms. In particular, an oil portrait of their cherished commander, Colonel Joseph Thoburn, hung prominently above the stage and moved the veterans to doff their hats in a show of respect to their fallen leader.[1]

As the reunion progressed, appointed speakers droned about the mundane business of the veterans' association. Most of the men in the crowd took little interest in these formalities and instead conversed with long lost friends, creating a buzz in the room. Against the backdrop of this scene, veterans carried the battle torn flags of the 1st West Virginia Infantry and Col. Joseph Thoburn's headquarters onto the stage and posted them behind the speaker. The bearers tenderly uncased the colors, unfurled and placed them in stands. The posting of the faded heirlooms hushed the crowd; now all eyes "gazed reverently on the tattered standards for which they had fought and bled and their comrades had died." Then, thunderous cheers spontaneously shattered the silence.

As the crowd roared in appreciation of the posting of the flags, Robert Strobel, the soldier who had born Thoburn's flag through many bloody battles such as New Market, Piedmont, Snickers Gap and Opequon Creek quietly walked into the room. He climbed onto the stage and stood in front of his former commander's colors. Overcome by evocative memories and the emotion of the moment, Strobel fell to his knees. He "buried his face in its smoke stained folds and gave entirely away to his feelings." Fellow veterans rushed to his side "until there was not a dry eye in the house." The organizers then adjourned the meeting as the somber remembrances reminded all that they were there to recollect and honor those who had made the ultimate sacrifice. Foremost among them in the eyes of these West Virginia veterans was Col. Joseph Thoburn.[2]

Colonel Thoburn's sword and scabbard, which were sent home to his family after he was killed on October 19, 1864. Suzanne Pezick Collection.

This flag might be Thoburn's headquarters flag from his time as a brigade and division command in the 1864 Shenandoah Valley Campaign and the same flag noted in this Introduction at the 1st West Virginia reunion.
Suzanne Pezick Collection.

∞ ∞

Joseph Thoburn was born April 28, 1825 at Carrickfergus near Belfast, in County Antrim, Northern Ireland. His ancestors had immigrated to Northern Ireland from Scotland. As staunch Protestants, the Thoburns fled their native land, rather than submit to worship God according to the dictates of King Charles I. The original family name was Thorburn, but the "r" was dropped in Ireland and the name became Thoburn.[3]

In the fall of 1825, the Colonel's father, Matthew Thoburn, uprooted his family and immigrated to North America. The family attempted to settle in Ohio, but Matthew's farming venture failed, so he moved his wife and two children to Germantown, Pennsylvania. Ultimately the Thoburn's returned to Ohio and planted permanent familial roots on a farm in Belmont County, not far from the Ohio River. There the family grew to ten children. Across the river in Virginia's northern panhandle lay the city of Wheeling, the region's economic center. In Ohio, young Joseph grew to manhood enlivened by his family's Christian faith and educated in the local public schools. Although limited economic opportunities did not allow him to continue formal schooling, Thoburn became a school teacher at age seventeen, a common stepping-stone toward higher professional aspirations in the nineteenth century. Within a few years, he advanced to principal of a local village school. While in that role, a local doctor tutored Thoburn on medicine to prepare him for medical school, his career aspiration. In 1848, he enrolled in Starling Medical School in Columbus, Ohio. He graduated in 1850 and moved to Brownsville, Pennsylvania, where he joined a private practice. In 1851, he received a lucrative appointment to the Ohio State Lunatic Asylum back in Columbus. Although he served diligently in the undemanding assignment, the administration he was part of fell out of political favor, which cost him his job in 1852. "Everyone who is in the least stained with Whiggery is decapitated," wrote Thoburn to his brother. "My head is off with the rest," he added, but "I leave here with the consciousness that my character and reputation is unsullied." In this position, Thoburn acknowledged that he possessed "every comfort that a man could ask to make me happy... I was a stranger to cares and anxieties except it was to know better how to execute the discharge of my duties." Undaunted, Thoburn moved to Wheeling, a burgeoning town with growing opportunities.[4] He observed:

> On every side it seems springing into life; new buildings are on every vacant spot springing up. Manufacturing and even commerce is being attracted here. And in a few weeks more we will have a direct rail road communication with the eastern cities and in another year a railroad connection to the west. Great things are promised for us. This is doubtless destined to be an important point.[5]

Amidst this boom-town environment, Thoburn started his own medical practice. He struggled to make ends meet, and times were so tough that his mother supplemented his meager income with "a little pittance." Nevertheless, at the end of 1852, he concluded that his resiliency in bouncing back from losing his position at the asylum and hard work in developing his Wheeling practice had developed "more energy and force of character than I could have acquired in Columbus." There he had been "more isolated from the world," while Wheeling provided him a larger "sphere of influence." He also concluded, "I am just poor enough to be stimulated to great exertions in order to sustain myself."[6]

On a personal perspective, Thoburn fully expected to marry and have a family of his own. He wrote "whenever I get rich and suitable material is available, I am bound to have a wife."[7] However, love bloomed before his bank account and medical practice realized his fiscal expectations. On December 13, 1853, Thoburn married Kate Ann Mitchell. The couple welcomed six-year old Gertrude Desal into their family home in 1854. "Gerty," an immigrant child from Germany, came to the Thoburns because her mother lacked the resources to care for all of her children. Two years later, the Thoburns experienced the birth of their first child, Anna Lyle. However, trial and tribulation followed as his medical practice struggled economically. To save money, Thoburn's family lived with relatives on a farm across the Ohio River. Although the distance was short and visits were frequent, he missed his family. Thoburn provided medical care to many of Wheeling's underprivileged residents. He well understood that there would be no recompense for much of his work but his strong Christian beliefs motivated his charitable work in spite of the drain it put on his family's finances. Within the span of one year, three of his patients died, prompting others to seek medical care elsewhere. One Wheeling woman haughtily observed that the financially struggling Thoburn "could not be much of a physician or he would have a horse and buggy like other physicians." Such criticisms did not affect him and he likely saw such things as unnecessary luxuries or "earthly" treasures that mattered naught in the larger scheme of life. Suddenly his prayers were answered and his dedication to his practice paid off. His finances improved to the point where the Thoburns rented a house in Wheeling and lived together as a family once again. But the happiness did not last long. Little Anna became sick and died in late September, bringing heartache to the family. "Our home is desolate, and her innocent prattle is sounding through the chambers of memory," wrote Thoburn. "Yet it is no more heard in our chambers. The pattering of her little footsteps is no more heard upon the floor, but these old

6   WORTHY OF A HIGHER RANK

*Thoburn married Kate Ann Mitchell
on December 13, 1853.
Suzanne Pezick Collection.*

*Left: Mrs. Thoburn, Anna Lyle, and Joseph Thoburn, circa 1856.
Right: Mrs. Thoburn holding Anna Lyle, circa 1856.
Suzanne Pezick Collection.*

familiar sounds seem now to be echoing back from the deepest recesses of the heart. In imagination, I seem now to behold her playing "bo peep" with me past the office door." Although heartbroken, his and Kate's devout faith pulled them through the challenging time. Even before she had passed, he confided to his journal, "But who can say it would not be best. The trial will do us good, and may not the education of heaven far exceed what we would or could give her here?"[8]

In spite of their grief, happiness was not far off. In January 1858, Kate gave birth to a healthy baby boy, Matthew Martin, who would be known as "Mattie" to family and friends. Two years later daughter Mary was born, and another daughter, Jennie, followed in 1862 during the war. His medical practice and income grew commensurately to keep pace with his now thriving family. People respected the charitable service he performed for Wheeling's poor and finally recognized that those efforts came at great personal cost to Doctor Thoburn. It was later written that Thoburn's charities "were almost as numerous as the days he lived and administered without pretension or ostentation."[9] Overall, a friend later remembered Thoburn as:

> One of the most amiable of men, modest, humble and unassuming… His mind was vigorous and well informed on all general subjects, but especially in his medical profession. He was a skillful and tender physician and paid particular attention to

Thoburn children: Mary, Jennie, and Matthew Martin. Suzanne Pezick Collection.

the poor. His moral character was without a single stain.[10]

Although life in general had been on a steady upswing for the Thoburn family, sectional strife changed everything as it did for most Americans in 1861. When the Southern states seceded from the Union, Thoburn sided strongly with the Union as did most residents in Wheeling, although tensions were high in the partisan border state atmosphere.[11]

Years before the advent of the Civil War, Thoburn prophetically opined that "the diabolical influence of slavery" would fracture the delicate balance of the United States.[12] Although a family man and a medical doctor, Thoburn dutifully enlisted as the regimental surgeon for the 1st [West] Virginia, United States Army.[13] At that time, everyone expected the war to be over quickly, likely decided by a single major battle, and consequently the initial terms of enlistment in the army spanned only three months. Thoburn's first combat experience came during the first organized land action of the war at the Battle of Philippi, West Virginia, on June 3, 1861. Although Thoburn was the regimental surgeon, his actions went far beyond the expectation of his official office. A fellow Virginian wrote home after the battle:

> None displayed more daring than did Dr. Thoburn, the Surgeon of the Regiment. Although his place was not to be in the fight at all, he was in the midst of it, on horseback and on foot, and firing as many guns as he could get hold of. … One of our boys said to me, that the Doctor was the most recklessly daring man he ever saw.[14]

Thoburn also treated his commander, Col. Benjamin F. Kelley who was among the few casualties that day. Although small, the battle proved to be a Union victory that denied Confederates control of northwestern Virginia. In turn, this permitted the region's Unionists to organize regiments and begin their march toward statehood unmolested by the secessionists.

On July 21, 1861, the Confederates won a decisive victory at the Battle of Manassas (Bull Run), but the North soldiered on and the end of the war was nowhere in sight. The Union authorities realized that the enlistment of men for a three-month tour of duty would not suffice to see the war through to victory. Consequently, a number of regiments reorganized to serve for three years, believing that would be enough time to win the war. The 1st West Virginia followed that course of action, and Thoburn ascended from the regimental surgeon to the rank of colonel commanding the new organization. The promotion was a testament to his innate leadership skills and integrity that he demonstrated while Col. Kelley recovered from his wounding at Philippi. When the other officers took leave of the regiment, Surgeon Thoburn assumed command, demonstrating his commitment to the regiment and the Union cause.[15]

Thoburn treated the severe wound of his commander, Colonel Benjamin F. Kelley, after the battle at Philippi. Photo courtesy of Richard A. Wolfe.

By early 1862, Thoburn and his regiment had joined the small force assembling under the command of Brig. Gen. Frederick W. Lander, operating along the Baltimore and Ohio Railroad. This rail line was a critical link between Washington, D.C. and the "western" states, and protecting it from Confederate raiders was of paramount importance if not the most glamorous military assignment.[16] Thoburn led his regiment

*Images from the wallet that Colonel Thoburn carried during the war.
Top, left: Mrs. Thoburn; Top, right: Matthew Thoburn (son).
Bottom, left: Mary Thoburn (daughter);
Bottom, right: Anna, daughter who died before the war. Suzanne Pezick Collection.*

in the minor action at Blue's Gap on January 7, 1862, where Confederates were driven away in confusion. The campaign shifted into the storied Shenandoah Valley, a locale that became the focus of Thoburn's Civil War service. General Lander died from disease before the active military campaign got underway, and Brig. Gen. James Shields assumed command. This campaign resulted in Thoburn's first major combat experience on March 23, 1862 at Kernstown, a village three miles south of Winchester. There, Union forces defeated Maj. Gen. Thomas J. "Stonewall" Jackson's Army of the Valley District. Jackson's men fought bravely from behind the shelter of a stone wall and repelled several Union attacks. At one point during the deadlock, Thoburn placed "his cap on the point of his sword and waving it to his men, called upon them to follow him in a dash across the open field and directly fronting the enemy's fire for the purpose of gaining a position on his flank."

The Mountaineer from Wheeling pushed his troops forward until struck down by a rebel minie ball. Undaunted by his wounds, Thoburn shouted to his men, "Go on and don't mind me, as I am not hurt," before crawling to the rear in search of a surgeon to treat his wounds. The 1st West Virginia failed in its attempt to flank the Confederate left, but Union commander Colonel Nathan Kimball, filling in for the previously wounded Shields, fed more regiments into the fight. With the sun going down, the Union troops finally routed Jackson's army from the battlefield, inflicting the only defeat Stonewall ever endured. The cost was high; more than 500 men were killed and wounded in the effort.[17]

Thoburn rode the Baltimore and Ohio Railroad home to Wheeling where he convalesced from his wound and spent a few weeks with his family. His former commander and now Brig. Gen. Benjamin F. Kelley joined him on the train at Ritchietown. He found Dr. Thoburn "in the mail car convenient to the water tank, nursing his arm as coolly as if it belonged to someone else." When Thoburn arrived at Centre Wheeling Station, the town's new found hero quickly attracted a crowd. Still wearing the same clothes that he was wounded in, admirers quickly noticed three bullet holes; one through his coat cape, another through the left leg of his pants, and the third through his arm which shattered the bone "just a little." Friends and acquaintances heartily welcomed Thoburn, and he "busied himself answering their desultory questions about the battle and the boys of the regiment." Back in the Valley, "the boys" of the 1st West Virginia anxiously awaited his return, "as a more devoted Colonel to the interests of his regiment never lived."[18]

While home on leave, Thoburn also received the congratulations of his commander, Col. Erastus B. Tyler. He wrote:

> I congratulate you, Sir, upon the soldierly and gallant conduct of yourself and command. Your conduct has won for you a place among the bravest of the brave defenders of our country's cause. I hope and trust Sir, the wound you received on that occasion may be speedily healed and you able soon again to assume command of your more than gallant regiment.[19]

Before his wound had fully healed, duty hastened Thoburn "back to the field, leaving behind him a beloved wife and three lovely children to whom he was ardently attached." He carried their photographs with him in a wallet throughout the war. He also carried the pledge that he made to Kate upon their marriage. It read, "My love for you will never die; I will keep it pure, untarnished and sacred; and will pray that it may be taken with me to the Paradise of God where I hope to greet you; and where, if God wills, I will love you always." One friend later recalled that Thoburn never entered battle without a prayer, something that would soon be needed in earnest as Stonewall Jackson was on the prowl with a reinforced army and was wreaking havoc in the Shenandoah Valley.[20]

Thoburn rejoined his command by late April in the valley. Now under the overall command of Maj. Gen. Nathaniel Banks, they pursued Jackson up the Shenandoah Valley and halted at Harrisonburg. However, Maj. Gen. George B. McClellan was clamoring for reinforcements for his effort to capture Richmond via the Peninsula Campaign, so the 1st West Virginia as part of Shield's division departed the Valley by the middle of May. They crossed over the Blue Ridge Mountains and joined Maj. Gen. Irvin McDowell's Army of the Rappahannock on the east side of that range. The troops marched through idyllic Warrenton in Fauquier County where "for the first time on our march in Virginia, the entire population, white and black, men, women and children were out to look at our brigade as it passed." The command marched on and bivouacked at a "beautiful encampment of wide rolling fields" near Catlett Station on the Orange and Alexandria Railroad. Shield's division ultimately joined McDowell at

Fredericksburg. Although his command had been slated to join McClellan, Jackson ran off a string of victories that prompted McDowell to march for the Valley.

The extensive marching in the Valley, and back and forth over the Blue Ridge tested the endurance of the troops. The regiment had logged over 400 miles in its travels but had seen no action since Kernstown. One West Virginian declared, "I stand it very well, and do not find fault for my health is good." His only complaint was "being burnt as black as an Indian" under the scorching Virginia sun. He further observed, "[for] Five days of our marching it did nothing but rain, and we had to ford streams and creeks without number." While most endured, the hard marches reduced the regiment's strength, as men physically broke down under the strain or became ill.[21]

With McDowell approaching the Valley from the east and additional Union reinforcements pouring in from the Alleghany Mountains to the west, Stonewall Jackson found himself in a precarious situation. To avoid being cut-off in the northern reaches of the Shenandoah, the cagey Virginian quickly marched southward and evaded the trap, falling back to the area east of Harrisonburg in the shadows of both the Blue Ridge and Massanutten Mountain near the village of Port Republic. There he waited to pounce on his pursuers. One column under Major General John C. Fremont had followed Jackson up the Valley Pike west of the Massanutten. Simultaneously, Thoburn marched with Shield's division up the muddy Luray Valley east of that range in hopes of trapping Jackson. But Stonewall turned on Fremont on June 8, defeating him at the battle of Cross Keys.

The next day, Jackson marched east and attacked the vanguard of Shields's force just north of Port Republic. Thoburn and the greatly outnumbered Union troops withstood several furious Confederate attacks, before Jackson overwhelmed the Federals with sheer numbers and brute force. After a valiant defense, the Union line crumbled, and the Confederates chased the Federals from the field in much confusion. Orders went out for the 29th Ohio to form the rear guard, but the Confederates quickly captured or scattered the Buckeyes, leaving the 1st West Virginia in the rear. As the Union troops left the battlefield, a horseless and hatless Thoburn trudged northward at the rear of the retreating column, believing a rear guard remained between his command and the Confederates. The Southern cavalry had charged up the road after dispersing the Ohioans and caught Thoburn by surprise. Belatedly jarred into action by a fellow West Virginia officer warning Thoburn of the danger, he ordered the men to wheel and fire, which they did dropping many Southerners from their saddles. A Confederate officer on a powerful iron-gray horse honed in on Thoburn and one of his captains, but both West Virginians fired their revolvers and shot him off his mount, ending the close call. The Union troops continued their retreat down the Luray Valley toward Front Royal, and Jackson's victory at Port Republic marked the end of the 1862 Valley Campaign. After a brief rest, Jackson marched over the Blue Ridge and joined Gen. Robert E. Lee in the defense of Richmond against McClellan's Army of the Potomac. Shields's troops and the other commands that had been bested by Jackson remained in the Shenandoah and Northern Virginia.[22]

Jackson's Valley Campaign had succeeded in drawing resources from the Union effort to capture Richmond, as an overly-cautious McClellan believed himself outnumbered and did not aggressively press his advance. In late June, Lee quickly turned and launched a series of vicious counterattacks that became known as the Seven Days' Battles. In the end, Lee's aggressiveness caused McClellan to withdraw, saving Richmond from what had seemed to be inevitable capture. (See Appendix A for a letter from Thoburn concerning this period) However, even before McClellan's defeat, President Abraham Lincoln had grown weary of the cautious McClellan and created a new army in Virginia that Lincoln hoped would take a more aggressive approach to the war. Thoburn's command and the other defeated forces from the Valley campaign formed the foundation of this new command. It was christened the Army of Virginia and placed under the command of Maj. Gen. John Pope of Illinois, an officer who had achieved marginal success in the western theater.

Although in a new army, Thoburn and the 1st West Virginia remained in the brigade of Col. Samuel Carroll, who had commanded them at Port Republic. On August 9, Pope ordered Carroll's brigade to the support of Gen. Banks, then engaged in combat with Stonewall Jackson's army at Cedar Mountain just south of Culpeper. Before they could join the fight, the Confederates drove Banks' corps from the field, and night brought an end to the battle, aside from desultory skirmishing and occasional artillery bursts. The campaign continued as a game of cat-and-mouse between the Union and Confederate forces between the Rappahannock and Rapidan Rivers. When Pope's entire army reached the scene Jackson withdrew southward until Lee arrived with the rest of the Army of Northern Virginia. Lee then proceeded to maneuver his army, forcing Pope to withdraw northward.

On August 17, Carroll's brigade conducted a reconnaissance toward the Rapidan River. Carroll and Thoburn crept through the underbrush along the river and spied the enemy position on the opposite bank through field binoculars. A Confederate sharpshooter saw the Federal officers, fired and hit Carroll in the chest, knocking him out of the campaign. Carroll's fall elevated Thoburn to brigade commander, a position he had temporarily held on occasion during the march to Port Republic. Now, he led the brigade in Pope's Campaign from central Virginia to Manassas. Thoburn soon became seriously ill, but the "excitement of battle" kept him upright in the saddle and out of the hospital until the combat had ceased.

On August 30 at Second Manassas, a Confederate attack had forced the Union army to withdraw. Thoburn's brigade fell back from the front lines for nearly a mile and halted in an open field near Pittsylvania mansion. Thoburn and his men thought they were in "perfect security" with another Union division posted between them and the enemy. His troops stacked arms and lounged about on the ground "talking about the fortunes of the day." Suddenly, a column of troops who belonged to Confederate Maj. Gen. A.P. Hill emerged from a pine thicket across the dim field. Thoburn could not positively identify these troops in the darkness but assumed they were friendly given his supposedly secure position. Uncertain, the ailing Thoburn ordered the brigade to arms, and called out "What troops are those?" A voice replied, "Secesh!" Still thinking that Union troops were supposed to be in his front, Thoburn shouted, "Don't talk that way or we'll give you a volley!" The voice yelled back, "Well, who are you?" Naively, Thoburn replied, "We are Union troops." A reply from across the field then called out, "Oh well then don't fire we're friends."[23]

Thoburn's new found "friends" quickly marched across the dark field in excellent order. Thoburn saw them and demanded, "If you are Union troops, wave your colors." They waved a captured U.S. battle flag, an act that relaxed Thoburn. The Southerners marched to within "15 steps" of Thoburn's line and then halted as if to stack arms. Thoburn galloped over to confer with their officers, but one Southerner fired, barely missing the Colonel and unveiling the ruse. He wheeled his horse around, and yelled to his men, "[It's] the enemy; fire!" An Indiana soldier of Thoburn's command reported, "At this instant a perfect sheet of flame proceeded from our ranks and from theirs. Simultaneous with the fire in front was another from our right flank, coming from a column that had slipped upon us unnoticed." The flanking column soon threatened to sever Thoburn's command from the bridge over Bull Run, so he ordered the men to break ranks and "get out of there as best we could." The command evaded capture in the darkness, hurriedly making its way eastward toward Bull Run and emerging in some disorder. As for Thoburn, the exigencies of battle and sickness had taxed him beyond the limits of human endurance. "He was perfectly prostrated when the battle was over," noted one of his men and was taken to the house of a senator in Alexandria, Virginia.[24]

Major Gen. John Pope.
Thoburn served under Pope in the ill fated
Second Bull Run Campaign during the summer of 1862.
Library of Congress.

When the 1st West Virginia returned home in October, Thoburn remained in Alexandria, "dangerously ill." Later in the month, he followed the regiment to Wheeling where he recuperated under the care of his wife and family. He arrived home in a very weak condition and recovered slowly. One month later, his illness still precluded him from resuming command. Finally, in December, he had recuperated enough to participate in a Court of Inquiry at Cumberland, Maryland. In the coming months, he would again take the field commanding a brigade responsible for guarding the Baltimore and Ohio Railroad and key Union outposts in West Virginia. These duties led to several minor engagements at places such as Moorefield, Petersburg, and other isolated mountain locales. Thoburn continued to perform this monotonous but necessary duty throughout 1863 until the spring of 1864.[25]

In January of 1864, the War Department solicited nominations for promotions to brigadier general from department commanders. The commander of the Department of West Virginia, Major General Benjamin F. Kelley, eagerly recommended Thoburn. Kelley wrote, "Col. Thoburn I regard as an accomplished officer and in every way worthy of a higher rank." Regardless, Thoburn and the budding state of West Virginia lacked the political influence to attain the star worn by many subpar generals, but military rank mattered little to Thoburn as long as he performed his assigned duty.[26]

Thoburn and the 1st West Virginia received leave in Wheeling after a difficult campaign in the mountains. The townspeople welcomed the regiment at the B & O Railroad Depot with "a lunch of sandwiches, hot coffee, apples and crackers." As the soldiers walked into the depot, a brass band greeted them with the patriotic strains of "Rally Round the Flag." Politicians couldn't help but get in on the act, as the governor and mayor both delivered "brief speeches" whose words have long since been forgotten. That same evening, the troops dined at Washington Hall in what was described as "the grandest affair of the kind which has taken place in the city." Among the attractions for the soldiers, "a bevy of young ladies" sang "Home, Sweet Home," which earned them "three of the heartiest and most unmistakable cheers we ever heard."

When supper ended, several dignitaries spoke at the podium, including Colonel Thoburn who offered his appreciation for the tremendous homecoming given his men. Thoburn downplayed his role in the war, but heaped praises upon his men who "had endured many hardships and faced terrible dangers for which they deserved much." At another meeting in March, Thoburn stood up to speak out on behalf of 200 men who had enlisted in the 1st West Virginia with the promise of a $200 bonus by Ohio County that had yet to be paid. "Justice demanded that these men should be paid," asserted Thoburn. He closed his speech with thoughts on the "hopeful and cheerful condition of the army and the confident and healthful tone among the people in regard to suppression of the rebellion." While the public events caught the local publicity, the most endearing part of the visit home for Thoburn was the time he spent with his wife and three children. The knowledge of the looming spring military campaign only made that time and the memories it created more endearing for Thoburn.[27]

Lincoln's appointment of Lt. Gen. U.S. Grant to overall command of the United States Army in 1864 initiated a period of unprecedented combat and casualties across all theaters of war. The rear echelon duty performed by the 1st West Virginia since the fall of 1862 had come to an end. Thoburn returned to the Shenandoah Valley, assigned to command a brigade under the hapless leadership of Maj. Gen. Franz Sigel. The coming campaign in the Shenandoah Valley saw more battles that were bigger and bloodier than any prior campaign in that region. The fighting began on May 15 at New Market and lasted more than five months, ending on until October 19 at Cedar Creek. During the course of this this campaign, Thoburn rose from brigade command to a firmly established division level leader by the time it ended. Personally, Thoburn always persevered to do his duty, but throughout the 1864 Shenandoah Valley Campaign, he found himself in several no-win situations attributable to the negligence or indiscretion of a superior officer.[28]

Foreword
by Bishop James M. Thoburn

My Brother, Colonel Joseph Thoburn, had ranked as a colonel but held the command of a major general in Gen. Sheridan's army at the time of his death. He was a brave true man, of strong character and had he lived no doubt have attained a high position in his adopted state of West Virginia. Many years afterward, I met President Rutherford B. Hayes who said to me, "Your brother was the best man I met in the whole course of the war." And in later years when a guest of the ex. President's family, I saw a group of photographs of officers who had been associated with him in the war, and was pleased to notice that he had given the place of honor at his right hand to my dear brother's picture. It was a singular fact in that two officers who served under my brother in that fateful campaign, both junior to him, both lived to become president of the United States, Rutherford B. Hayes and William McKinley.[29]

Bishop James M. Thoburn. The World's Work, Doubleday, Page, and Co., New York, 1909.

Editor's note: Although Hayes and McKinley were Thoburn's comrades in the Army of West Virginia during the 1864 Valley Campaign and certainly interacted with him on a regular basis, they never served in a subordinate role to him.

1

The New Market Campaign

In the spring of 1864, Lt. Gen. Ulysses S. Grant developed a grand strategy to put Union armies on the offensive across the South. In Virginia, Grant personally accompanied the Army of the Potomac in its campaigns against General Robert E. Lee's Army of Northern Virginia. In West Virginia, the Lincoln administration had placed Major General Franz Sigel in command of that department. Sigel had a poor reputation as a military commander, but was popular in the burgeoning German community in the North, an important factor in 1864, a presidential election year. In spite of the German's shortcomings as a commander, Grant reasoned that Sigel "could hold a leg while someone else skinned." Unfortunately, Sigel couldn't maintain a firm grasp on the situation, and his campaign in the Shenandoah Valley turned into failure at the battle of New Market.[30]

In this campaign, Thoburn commanded an infantry brigade composed of the 1st and 12th West Virginia, 54th Pennsylvania, and 34th Massachusetts regiments. Thoburn reported to Brig. Gen. Jeremiah Sullivan of Indiana who commanded Sigel's infantry while Maj. Gen. Julius Stahel led the cavalry. Sigel's army numbered about 8,500 men who soon confronted 5,000 Confederates from the Shenandoah Valley and Southwest Virginia under the command of Maj. Gen. John C. Breckinridge, former Vice President of the United States under President James Buchanan and the Southern Democratic candidate for

President in 1860.

When the battle occurred on May 15, Thoburn's brigade bore the brunt of the infantry fighting for the Union and suffered heavy losses. After an uncoordinated counterattack, Thoburn covered the retreat from the battlefield as the army withdrew down the Shenandoah Valley to its camps at Belle Grove plantation along the banks of Cedar Creek between Middletown and Strasburg.

Thoburn's diary for this period captures the anticipation for Grant's spring campaign to begin and the appetite in Sigel's army for information about the epic encounter between Grant and Confederate General Robert E. Lee. Thoburn's writings provide good details on the activities in the Valley and also reveal the impetuous nature of Sigel's orders. Thoburn also records reports from other campaigns as they come in revealing the often sketchy information that came out through the newspapers of the day.

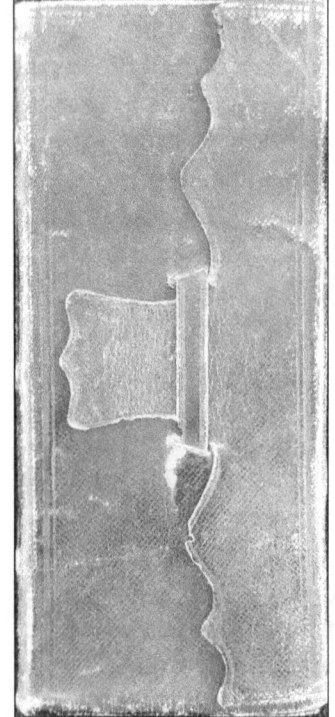
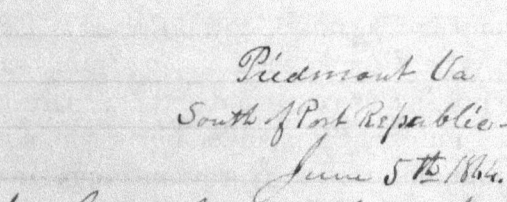

Left: Colonel Thoburn's diary.
Above: an excerpt from the diary,
on the date of the Battle of Piedmont,
June 5, 1864.
Suzanne Pezick Collection.

May 4, 1864: Near Winchester, Va. rec'd letter from West Virginia Governor Arthur I. Boreman in relation to Lt. J. M. Doudy, attended to. Rec'd a letter informing me that Brother David is dangerously ill. Brother Thomas promoted to a Lieutenancy. No word from our army. If movements are about taking place they are very quietly done. This command is in expectation of an early move.[31]

Thoburn's brother, Thomas C. Thoburn, rose to the rank of 2nd lieutenant in the 50th Ohio Infantry, serving in Gen. William T. Sherman's 1864 Atlanta Campaign. In 1865, he subsequently served as major in the 196th Ohio Infantry. Suzanne Pezick Collection.

May 5th: A warm day. The cavalry are reported to have had a skirmish yesterday with the enemy at Strasburg - reports in our favor but not important. A small force of rebel cavalry made a demonstration last night upon Martinsburg and some captures are reported to have been made.

May 6th: It is reported that some rebel cavalry have dashed into Piedmont [WV] and destroyed the machine shops and rail road property at that place. My Brigade was out on drill and performed well, i.e. considering inexperience in such movements. Baltimore paper of the 4th and 5th Rec'd; no news of importance from the Army. We are expecting to hear daily of [Gen. U.S.] Grant moving.[32]

May 8th: Near Winchester. The *Baltimore American* rec'd last night gives a report that the Army of the Potomac is in motion and had crossed the Rapidan [River]. A column was also said to be moving up the Peninsula and another on the South side of the James River. It is also reported that all the rebel force in Western Virginia has been withdrawn. If this be so, there is no further need for us here. I hope we may be moved before long. P.M, Orders to march just Rec'd. We move tomorrow at 6 A.M. This order will give satisfaction to officers and men. Visited the nurseries and flower gardens of Mr. Steel immediately west of Winchester. The ravages of war have not touched him; his gardens and surroundings are beautiful. There is a great deal of wealth in Winchester and a Horticulturist and florist so near can't help having a lucrative business. Mr. Steel is an old Scotchman and professes to be loyal but his loyalty is of that quiet sort that strives to give no offence to the "Secesh".

Yesterday's *Baltimore American*, rec'd today, confirms the fact of a general forward movement of all our armies. [Maj. Gen. William T.] Sherman in three columns is moving forward on Dalton, [Georgia]. The probabilities would seem to be strong in favor of success to the Union Armies. In smaller engagements the rebels have rather been the gainers since early spring. But Lt. Gen'l Grant seems to have been more eager thus far in preparing for a grand movement of the whole army than to protect and strengthen all the smaller points. This should be the wiser policy and the trifling loss of a few small outposts and will be amply repaid by the greater gains of large and more decisive victories on our part.

May 9th: Near Winchester, Va, 7 A.M. Everything is in readiness for our forward move. My Brigade takes the advance. Morning fair and pleasant.

Cedar Creek Bridge, 4 miles from Strasburg. 4 P.M. Arrived at this place at 1 P.M. and went into camp, the immediate neighborhood is rough but the soil continues of the same quality as the lower end of the valley. Some of the best farms I have seen in the Valley are this side [south] of Kernstown. No enemy seen or heard of. Reports came into camp before stating of a great battle and victory over Lee, but the rumor has no authentic foundation. The rebels on the road have reports of an opposite character of a defeat to Grant's forces. We are all in a state of intense anxiety to hear the results of last week's movements.

May 10th: Cedar Creek 6 A.M. The Report of a battle between Grant and Lee is confirmed and also the defeat of the latter. There are also rumors of a force of the enemy approaching us. An unknown force is said to be at Woodstock with pickets within seven or eight miles of us. A skirmish with some of Mosby's cavalry was had yesterday, advantage in our favor. By order of Gen'l Sigel no mail matter will be permitted to be carried between this [place] and Martinsburg. 9 P.M. Orders are issued to move tomorrow morning at 6 o'clock. The *Baltimore American* of yesterday is rec'd. The news from the Army of the Potomac is very indirect and not satisfactory. The sum of it is that after two days hard fighting Grant had stood his ground and the enemy had ceased to confront him. This will be a stirring week.[33]

May 11th, 1864: Near Woodstock VA. Arrived here this P.M. at 2 o'clock, raining heavy. Rebel cavalry were driven out of this place. Generals Thomas Rosser and John D. Imboden are said to be but a few miles beyond. The citizens here have rebel news to the effect that Lee had defeated Grant and that the latter was in retreat. This is doubtful. The country has been quite hilly from Strasburg here, and comparatively undisturbed by army operations so far as fencing is concerned. Along the line of pike in places the fence is gone but the absence of fence is the exception. The country people along the way seem tired of the war and would willingly come back under the Union. A report has come in that a portion of our cavalry was defeated yesterday near Wardensville. No particulars are known. *Baltimore American* of 10th rec'd and statements therein claim great successes for Grant. Butler is also said to be operating successfully South of the James River.[34]

May 12, 1864 1 mile N. of Woodstock. Rainy day - *Baltimore American* rec'd. The report of a victory over Lee is confirmed. Butler is also reported to have defeated Beauregard at Petersburg. And Sherman is fighting in Northern Georgia. Our sky is brightening. The President has officially announced that success in a Proclamation calling upon the people to render thanks to Almighty God and implore the continuance of his favor until the struggle is completed.

Per contra [on a small scale], Breckinridge is reported to be moving down the valley for the purpose of driving us out. A rebel force of about 800 is reported in our immediate front and they picket the valley so effectually that no information can reach us from above them.[35]

May 13, 1864: Near Woodstock. One Regiment was today sent down to Edenburg accompanied by a section of Capt. John Carlin's Battery.[36] Another regiment was sent over to the mountain road in the direction of Wardensville. And four companies went out to Columbia Furnace; one hundred cavalry accompanied each command. They are to return this evening. Rec'd letter from my wife, the first since the 29th of April.

May 14, 1864: Rain still continues. The troops that were sent out yesterday have returned - nothing was seen. Our cavalry have all gone to the front today. Grant is reported to have had another very hard fought battle without decisive results.[37] Gen'l Warren was killed.[38] No particulars. The road to Richmond is a hard one. If Grant succeeds it will be at the expense of a heavy sacrifice.

At 9 A.M., the First W.Va. and 34th Mass. have been ordered to Mt. Jackson with the 1st Brigade. I remain here with two regiments. 9 P.M. It has rained all afternoon and is still raining. Streams will be so high that movements may stop. Slight cannonading was heard in the direction of Mt. Jackson, where we have two regiments, and a battery. The whole command moves forward tomorrow morning at 4 o'clock. *Baltimore American* of the 13th rec'd. The fighting is reported to be terrific and slaughter immense. Grant continues to press Lee who has fallen back beyond the "Po" [River].

*Captain John Carlin.
1st West Virginia Light Artillery, Battery D. "Carlin's Battery."
Richard A. Wolfe Collection.*

May 17, 1864: Strasburg, Va., Left Woodstock on the morning of the 15th with two regiments of infantry for the front. Col. Moor engaged the enemy all morning with artillery and also some infantry skirmishing but without any decisive results and without loss on our side. Arriving at Mt. Jackson I was ordered into camp with two Regiments of Moor's Brigade.[39] This was about 11 AM. At 12 M., an order came to send forward one regiment of infantry to escort [a] battery to the front. After marching a mile this order was countermanded and I was directed to move all the infantry back to the high ground between the Shenandoah and Strong Creek and there remain until further orders.

In half an hour I rec'd orders to move to the front as rapidly as possible with two regiments of infantry. Moor had the day before moved forward to New Market where he was still holding his ground. I made the six miles forward in a little over an hour. Marching my men since morning 30 miles. When I arrived on the ground the enemy was

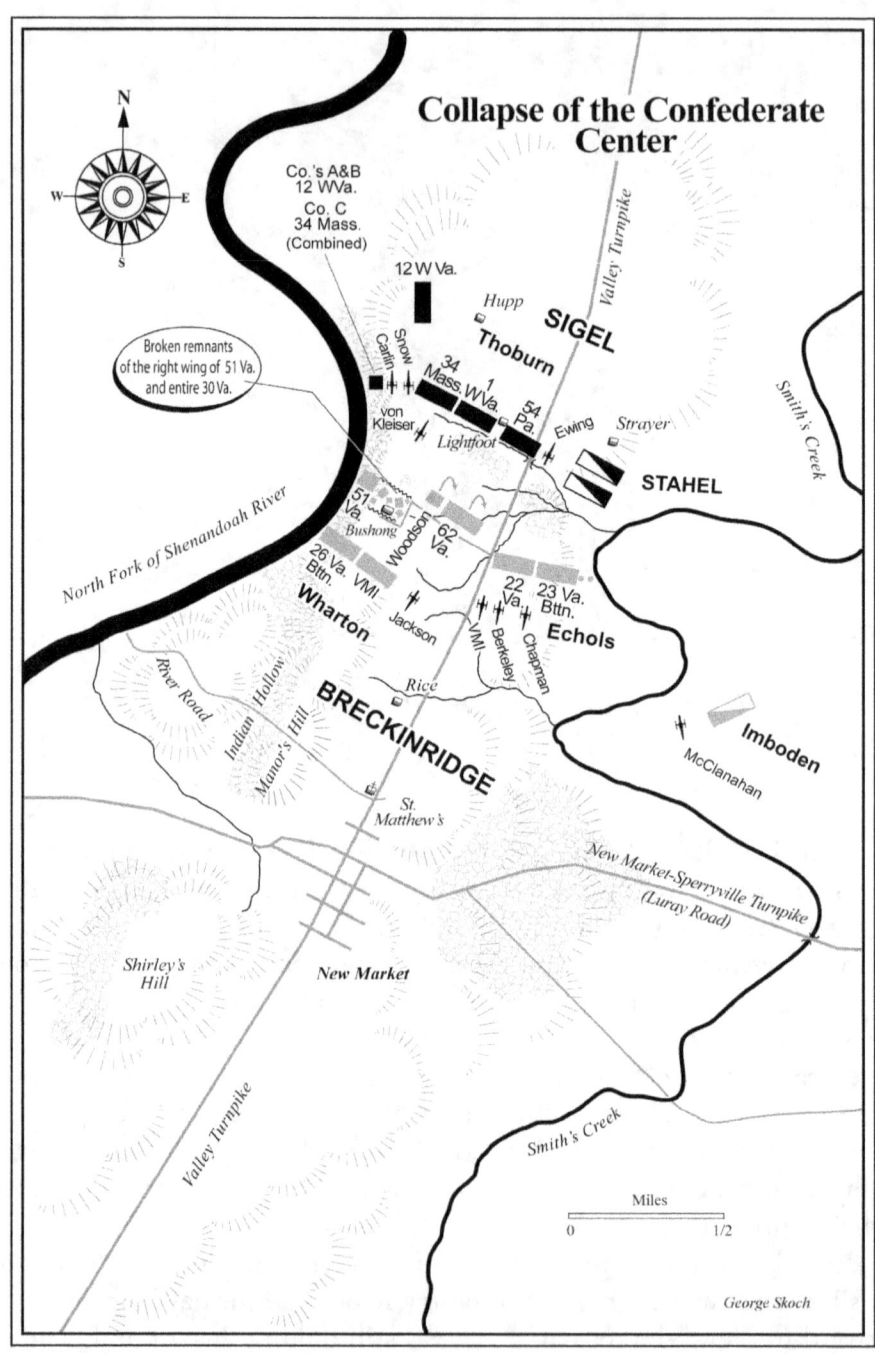

The Battle of New Market, May 15, 1864.
Map courtesy of Charles R. Knight and Savas Beatie Publishing.

advancing upon us in line of battle. Our skirmish line was gradually falling back. I found the two regiments that had been on the ground all morning in position in a little ravine about 250 paces in the rear of another line of regiments which were also posted in a ravine.

I was instructed to put my two Regiments in line with the two previously on the ground. Carlin's Battery was on the right and the last of my regiments was moving into line to the right of the battery when the enemy opened upon the first line of the 1st Brigade [Moor's]. This line immediately yielded and poured back through our second line.

I immediately advanced my line out of the ravine so that I could rake the enemy as they emerged from the [first] ravine. In front, the 1st W.Va pressed forward in the center with a shout, the 34th Mass. on their right and the 54th Pa. on their left. The 1st in their eager zeal pressed forward of the line to their right and left and received the first galling fire from the enemy and seeing themselves in front of the line fell back and made a good stand. The 34th Mass. and the 54th Pa. did nobly. No troops could have fought better but the enemy's line gradually enveloped our flanks and we had to give way.[40]

The 12th W.Va. as a reserve was not actively engaged and fell back with the other regiments. Three regiments of rebel infantry emerged from the woods on the hill to our right and poured in a raking fire that threw our men into confusion and caused the loss of three pieces of artillery from Carlin's battery. From the [other] batteries three pieces were also captured. We fell back beyond the Shenandoah and destroyed the bridge. After nightfall, we continued the retreat and arrived at this place yesterday evening. On the 15th and the night of the same day the 54th Pa. marched 44 miles in 22 hours and in addition stood the very hardest of the fight. The 12th W.Va. in the same time marched 41 miles. The loss of the 1st W.Va. 81 in killed, wounded, and missing. That of the 12th W. Va. – 46; the 54th Pennsylvania - 174 and the 34th Mass. 224. Of these 60 were killed.

Our troops were posted in a very poor manner and were too much divided. A portion of the command had marched 20 miles before going into action and were not 10 minutes on the ground before they were engaged. Better positions were in the rear of what we occupied and if the troops in front had fallen back two miles we could have held our ground against more than opposed us. And had our force been brought into play together, the enemy would have been defeated. As it was they fought two regiments, which broke and ran with the first fire. Then the second line of three regiments held them beautifully in check for some time doing good work with their rifles. Several times the enemy's lines wavered as if about giving way but finally our forces had to yield. My horse was shot under me but I escaped without a scratch, to allay our grief over our loss we have the gratifying intelligence that Grant is successful with the Army of the Potomac.[41]

May 18th: Cedar Creek - Strasburg. The 34th Mass and the 12 W.Va. were moved out today and posted on Fisher's Hill 2½ miles beyond Strasburg. The news from Grant is that recent rains have so swelled the streams that the pursuit of Lee for the present is abandoned. The previous accounts of the successes of the Army of the Potomac are confirmed. Two letters rec'd from my wife. All are well.

P.M. A report has been received at Head Quarters that Lee's army is retreating in the direction of Lynchburg. This is incredible. It would be giving up Virginia to us and the Confederacy is not ready for this. Their reverses are not great enough to warrant such a step.

May 19th: Cedar Creek, Va. near Strasburg. Last night Gen'l Jeremiah Sullivan together with the commanding officers of brigades, regiments and batteries made a complimentary call upon Gen'l Julius Stahel and passed a very pleasant hour at his quarters. The bands of the 15th and 21st New York [Cavalry Regiments] were present. The command that was sent out to Fisher's Hill this morning was ordered back to Strasburg to take position in the entrenchments there.[42] Was appointed today field officer of the day in chief for five days - will be kept busy.[43]

*Major Gen. Franz Sigel.
Sigel's tactics at the Battle of New Market wasted his manpower
advantage and caused his army to be defeated in detail.
Library of Congress.*

2

The Battle of Piedmont and Capture of Staunton

After the battle of New Market, Gen. Robert E. Lee had urged the Confederate commander in the Shenandoah, Maj. Gen. John C. Breckinridge to go the offensive and chase Sigel to Maryland. He objected and instead took his force to join Lee in the defense of Richmond. Grant promptly relieved Sigel of command and replaced him with Maj. Gen. David Hunter, who quickly had the U. S. Army of the Shenandoah advancing in the Valley toward the vital Virginia Central Railroad which linked the Valley to Richmond and Lee's army. Hunter's prompt action caught the Confederacy off-guard, and Lee ordered Brig. Gen. William E. "Grumble" Jones to bring troops from Southwest Virginia and East Tennessee to resist Hunter's advance. Jones barely arrived in time using the railroads to quickly transfer his troops over a long distance.

Hunter defeated Jones in the Battle of Piedmont and marched into Staunton where he proceeded to destroy shops and warehouses and seriously damaged the Virginia Central Railroad throughout the area. After Hunter's victory at Piedmont, General Robert E. Lee returned Maj. Gen. John C. Breckinridge's small division to the Shenandoah Valley to dispute Hunter's further advance. Thoburn's journal reveals his personal assessments of his commanding officers, observations about the Valley and its people as well as his thoughts on the changing conduct of war in the Valley.

May 22: Strasburg, Va, Maj. Gen'l. Sigel was relieved yesterday by Maj. Gen'l David Hunter. I rejoice at the change; Hunter will be a very poor Gen'l indeed if he is not better than Sigel. The latter is a well-informed military man, honest and devoted to our cause, but he lacks the practical common sense that enables a man to adapt himself to circumstances. He has courage; still he becomes flurried when in action and his orders are not clear and prompt. I feel kindly toward the Gen'l - yet I would rather he would never have another command.

Gen'l Hunter has some reputation as a military man. He appears to be very energetic and active. Yet, I would rather have seen make a better start. To begin with, his first general order promising the men half rations and mule meat was not wise. Men can endure a great deal but they should not be promised the worst until we get to the worst. He required the command to move this morning, every man carrying an extra pair of shoes, and many of the men are without any shoes at all and none to be had. He ordered one hundred rounds of ammunition to be carried in the knapsack when there is not a knapsack in the command. All having been left at Martinsburg, and there is not one hundred rounds of ammunition to the man to be had.[44]

All this only proves that he has spoken too fast. He begins to work before he knows the material he has to work with. Still I like his energy and if he has some military judgment on the field we may do very well. Our movement into the interior with a small force is hazardous, and requires a very discreet as well as bold commander.

During the last twenty-four hours parties of rebel cavalry have been hovering around our picket posts at one place, capturing eleven men and forty horses. Moved Head-quarters about half a mile into the edge at a fine grove. Gen'l Hunter is hurrying up every preparation for an early movement. We will not be here longer than three days.

May 24, 1864: Cedar Creek, near Strasburg, Va. Rec'd information this morning that John Thoburn was killed in a railroad accident near Grafton. The car ran off the track killing two and wounding thirty. Poor John! But more to be pitied, his poor family. Preparations are going forward for an early move. We expect to be moving tomorrow morning.

May 25, 1864: A heavy rain last night. This morning bright, cool and pleasant. The enemy quiet around us. Orders to move not yet rec'd.

May 26th: Cedar Creek, Move this morning at 9 A.M. in the direction of Staunton. The *Baltimore American* of yesterday rec'd this morning reports another battle with Lee in which the enemy was worsted and is in retreat towards Richmond. On our present move, our men carry half rations and propose subsisting on the country for the full ration. A heavy rain last night. This morning cloudy and cool.

1 1/2 miles North of Woodstock, 8 P.M. The command went into camp at this place at 5 o'clock this P.M. Nothing unusual occurred during the march. No news from the enemy in our front. It is said that Rosser is somewhere in the valley. My impression is that we are attempting to form a junction with Gen'l [George] Crook who may be coming in this direction or in the direction of Staunton where we may be attempting to form a junction with him.[45]

Gen'l Hunter has issued an order to burn the houses in every neighborhood where guerrilla bands molest our troops or trains in passing. In accordance with this order two dwellings were burnt today on the line of our march. I deeply regret such a course. It can do us no good and is sure to bring us to disgrace and justly too. The innocent will be made to suffer and instead of favoring a return of Union Sentiment, the inhabitants will become more incensed against us.[46]

We are here with four days rations only and are informed that it must last ten days. The consequence is that we must subsist on the country. This will lead to many irregularities on the part of the men. Discipline will become lax and the moral tone of the command will go down. I hope my fears may not be realized. From my heart, I pity the poor inhabitants of the country through which we pass. Do the best we can, property will be destroyed and the innocent will suffer. War is a terrible scourge and how great the crime of creating such a war as ours! Could the end have been seen from the beginning, surely the authors would have turned from their evil purpose!

May 27th: Three years ago this day the 1st W. Va. Inf. left Wheeling on the Baltimore and Ohio R. R. That morning was wet and raining like this. The men were citizens then - soldiers now. Foraging parties are being sent out today to gather supplies for commissary stores. Re-enforcements are said to be on the way to join us.

May 28th: The foraging parties yesterday brought in about half rations for one day. Prospect for provisions up the valley not good, the valley is bare of subsistence. Morning bright and clear; will not move before tomorrow.

4 P.M. Orders are out to move early tomorrow morning. Our foraging parties have been busy today and have failed to supply the command with half rations. Provisions are more scarce above, and as we go farther up [south] the valley, we will fare worse. The system of foraging that has been adopted is very defective in that each command forages for itself, and the cavalry having greater facilities pick up the greater share leave the infantry to suffer [for want of food]. Again the party that is in the advance gets all that is within reach and those that follow have to send parties far into the country for their share. The better way would be to have all stores collected and an equal distribution made by the proper officers. Then all would fare equally and there would be less complaining. Our column moves tomorrow morning with half rations. When we go into camp, the men will be without rations, and it will be the evening of the following day before supplies can be gathered so that 24 hours will be passed without food.

May 29th: Rude's Hill, near New Market. Left Woodstock this morning at 5 o'clock. Arrived here at 2 P.M. Day very pleasant. A squad of rebel soldiers were here when we approached. Visited the battlefield of two weeks ago. Saw quite a number of our wounded. And the graves of our dead - Poor fellows - their bodies were stripped and thrown into a hole and but half buried.

Our men have marched on less than half rations. They have to move tomorrow morning on the same rations. They know that Gen'l Hunter has issued an order that they must subsist on the country and license of this kind has no limits when in the hands of every one. I am ashamed of the conduct of the men and have done all in my power to prevent pillaging in my command. I was never with an expedition [that] I disliked like this.

May 30th: Rude's Hill. The command does not move today. The wounded that were left here are being attended to and the killed properly covered. They were nearly all piled into one hole and we have made a mound of earth over them and covered it with sod. Gen'l Sullivan has turned his energies to the suppression of pillaging and will be successful so far as the infantry is concerned. Gilmor and McNeil were in the neighborhood last night.[47] Breckinridge left here for Staunton on the 17th. Imboden is above us somewhere. A train from Martinsburg to this place was captured by the enemy last night near Newtown. The report is that the general com'd'g. [Hunter] has ordered the town to be laid in ashes [burned].

May 31st: Rude's Hill. We do not move today. No news today from anywhere. Foraging parties unsuccessful yesterday in obtaining full supplies. Everything in the country (which is not much) has been moved out of our reach by the inhabitants. They have had timely warning of our approach and as we move farther up we will find less and less. We are expecting to join Crook's command before long. Our wounded that are in New Market are doing well and are well cared for. The citizens have been very kind.

June 1, 1864: Rude's Hill. A sultry day. No word from the enemy. Expect to move tomorrow morning. No word from the Rail Road or from Grant. The rebels have no news either. They say the railroad and telegraph wires are cut.

June 2nd: Harrisonburg. Left Rude's Hill this A.M. at 5 o'clock. Enemy's picket was discovered at Lacey Springs. And Imboden was found at this place, but he left without offering us battle. Breckenridge is reported to be in the direction of Buffalo Gap ready to operate against Gen'l Crook who is thought to be coming in that direction. This is a very pretty little village. Many of our wounded were found here and they have fared kindly at the hands of the citizens. A Richmond paper of the 30th rec'd. They are still driving Grant who is now within nine miles of the City. With an appearance of sincerity, Grant is said to be driven out of the wilderness.[48]

June 3rd: I met Col. Gray today and other citizens who have been kind to our wounded. My interview with them was pleasant. Why is it that those of the same flesh and blood, the same principles and living in the same land cannot be one people? David Irwin a Presbyterian clergyman of this place, has two brothers and a mother and sister living in Wheeling who are all warm friends of the Union while he is such a bitter secessionist that when his nephews called on him this morning, he told them he did not know whether he ought to shake hands with them. He inquired for his mother, but did not ask for his sister and brothers. Thus he lets his humanity and Christianity give way to the unholy cause of secession.[49]

The German element in this county is said to be friendly to the Union, and we are told by some parties that the overthrow of Lee's Army by Grant would be hailed with satisfaction by a great many prominent citizens. Enthusiasm for the rebel cause was manufactured this spring by getting up the impression that the Yankees were about giving up, and that this was to be the last year of the War. To get done with this war, a great many will lend themselves more willingly to it. But when they see that Grant moves toward Richmond, and that the Union Army everywhere, with the exception of Louisiana, is penetrating deeper and deeper into their territory they will see the falsity of the expectation of conquering the Union Army this year.[50] And they have had the admission in the Richmond papers that the Confederacy will not be able to endure another year. So that but a few months more are needed to manifest to them the hopelessness of their cause.[51]

Rebel pickets are within two or three miles of us. Another day or two will develop what we will be able to do. If we succeed in making a junction with Crook, all will be well. If not it will be disastrous. We are getting about one-half rations of flour and full rations of beef from the country. Tomorrow our supply of coffee and sugar runs out. The men will feel this loss very much. Should the enemy encroach closely upon us, we will be cramped very much for subsistence. And should we have to make a hurried retreat, we will go back starving for we have cleaned [out] the country over which we have passed. But I hope a better fate is in store for us.

June 4th: Port Republic, Va. 8 P.M. Left Harrisonburg this A.M. at 5 o'clock. Arrived here at 1 P.M. The whole afternoon was consumed in laying a pontoon train and crossing the river. When the train was laid it was found to be incapable of supporting the weight of a loaded wagon and the wagons with the artillery had to be taken a mile down the river and across the ford.

The country from Harrisonburg [to] here is not in appearance equal to that further down the valley. The limestone is in some places replaced by a slate formation and the pine, in such places, is more vigorous than the oak. The land is however, capable of a higher state of cultivation. From New Market [to] here the farms are but poorly improved, and I would scarcely desire better farming land. We found the citizens along the line of our march apprised of our coming, and they had the cattle and horses all driven away to prevent them [from] falling into our hands. We found all the male inhabitants capable of bearing arms away from home. Their families say they have lately been pressed into the Army. And from what we can learn along the road, the majority have gone in much against their will, and we have many friends in the rebel army.[52]

Gen'l Hunter's movement in this direction is a very bold one. Gen'l Crook is said to be on the other side of Staunton. Instead of attempting to form a junction with him we have moved away from him. If the enemy should be stronger than our divided force the consequence may be fatal to us, if advantage is taken of it [by the Confederates]. The enemy may throw himself upon our detachment and defeating that rapidly, turn and defeat the other. The night is rainy and disagreeable. Day after tomorrow it will be two years since I came to this piece under Gen'l Shields.[53]

June 5th: Port Republic, Va. We move this morning at 4 1/2 o'clock - morning damp. Through the fault of the chief commissary no ration of beef was issued last night and only one-fifth of a ration of flour. Quite an amount of stores were taken yesterday, and such dereliction of duty will, I fear, go unpunished. It is a bad condition in which to go forth to meet the enemy, as we expect to. Such management does not promise well for effective results.

June 5th: Piedmont, Va., South of Port Republic. We have had a hard fought battle and by the favor of God we have been victorious. The enemy were strongly posted at this place and made a strong fight. We engaged them this morning at 9 A.M. and at 4 P.M. Thoburn's 2nd

Brigade made a final and triumphant charge and drove the enemy from the field taking one thousand prisoners and capturing three stands of colors. The 1st Brigade had made two unsuccessful attacks upon the front of the enemy but were repulsed. I was then directed to move upon the flank of the enemy's line, which compelled it to give way at once. The men of the Brigade behaved gallantly and I had the great satisfaction of having the conduct of the Brigade commended by everyone I met.

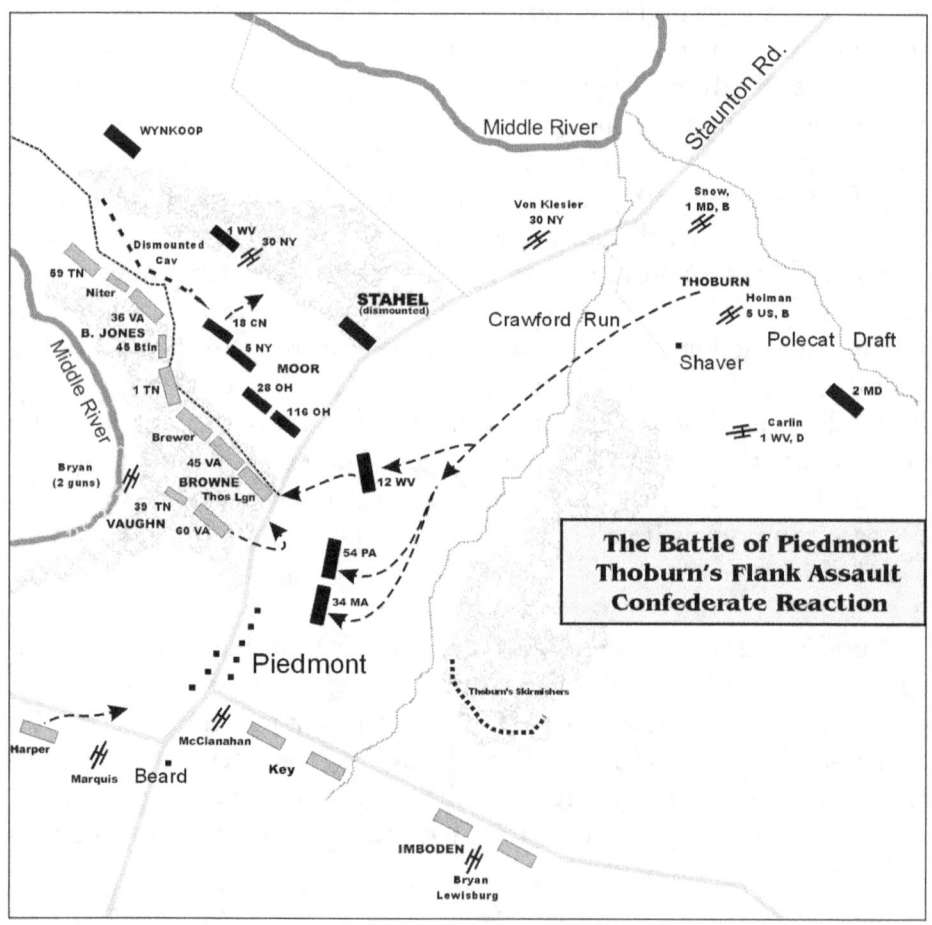

The Battle of Piedmont
Thoburn's Flank Assault
Confederate Reaction

June 6th: Stanton, Va. We left Piedmont this AM at 5 o'clock and arrived here after the middle of the day. The enemy were not to be found. The disorganized force has retreated in the direction of Waynesboro. Many stragglers were picked up from there and it is believed that at least one-thousand of those engaged are now hiding from the rebel authorities to prevent being again taken into the rebel army. On the way from Piedmont [to] here [Staunton] we found about one half of the families who gave evidence or sympathy and good will towards us. If a proper rule was exercised over the people of this country one half of them would be outspoken friends of the Union at once. Staunton is a very pretty place. Its two asylums, the Lunatic and the Deaf and Dumb are splendid buildings with beautiful surroundings.

The 1st W. Va. was first to enter town, which she did carrying under her own colors [and] the inverted battle flag of the 31st Rebel Virginia, which she captured yesterday.[54] Ours is the first Union force that ever entered this town. We expect to be joined in a few days by a force from the Kanawha under Generals Crook and [William W.] Averell. If we are permitted to remain here until this junction is formed, our force will

View of the Piedmont battlefield from the low ground near Hunter's headquarters. Thoburn led his brigade through the field past the ground where the nearest trees are in the middle distance on the left of the photo. He moved 500 yards beyond this point, faced his brigade to the right and then advanced up the slope and attacked toward the clump of trees in the center atop the high ground. This was the location of the exposed flank of the Confederate left wing during the battle.

be strong enough to maintain itself here against anything that the enemy is likely to send against us.⁵⁵

From rebel sources, we receive information that Crook had a fight a few days ago with Mudwall Jackson and was victorious.⁵⁶ Richmond papers of the 4th inst. are rec'd. Some hard fighting is reported to have taken place between Grant and Lee [at Cold Harbor] with the advantage all in Lee's favor. [Gen. Joseph E.] Johnston is also reported to be repelling all the advances made by Sherman who they claim has lost 45,000 men since he commenced his forward movement and that the remnant of his army is in a starving and demoralized condition.⁵⁷

To read their paper one would suppose that success was everywhere on the side of the rebels and defeat and disaster everywhere ours. They do not attempt to explain why it is that our columns continue to advance upon every side of them. Their tone is confident and hopeful and thus their people are deceived concerning the state of affairs in the Confederacy. We are subsisting entirely on the country and the poor people tell us they are starving, while but little can be found on the premises of the rich. We will be unable to remain long in one place, and if we are joined by Crook and Averell, we must either continue to move or starve.

June 7th: Staunton, Va. Started this morning for Buffalo Gap expecting to bag a rebel force under Mudwall Jackson, but they had left last night, and after marching 4 miles we ascertained this to be a fact and returned to our old camp. Jackson has moved South of Staunton to make a junction with Imboden at Waynesboro. Richmond papers of the 5th rec'd. Great accounts are given of a victory over Grant.⁵⁸

7.P.M. A scout has arrived, in camp from Averell who was 15 miles from here yesterday noon. A junction of our forces will be formed tomorrow morning and then we will expect to be strong enough to hold the valley against any force to be brought against us.

June 9th: Staunton, Va. The commands of Gen'ls Crook and Averell arrived here yesterday, a regiment of our Cavalry were driven back by the enemy two miles this side of Waynesboro. We are expecting to move upon that place before long.⁵⁹

View of the Piedmont battlefield. This picture is taken from the high ground looking east toward the Blue Ridge Mountains. Thoburn's attack struck the clump of trees in the right distance (the last discernable tree line in the photo backdropped by the mountains) and rolled up the Confederate line. The Confederate battle line ran from the lower left of this photo at the base of the hill and extended diagonally toward the clump of trees. The line can be traced by following the line of shrubs that conceals a fence line until it is lost in the woods in the middle distance of the photo. The line extended to the distant clump of trees. Most of this area was wooded at the time of the battle and a farm lane ran along the northern edge of the woods where the concealed fence line is situated.

Corporal Joseph Halstead carried the battle flag of the 12th West Virginia over the Confederate breastworks at Piedmont in the final, victorious charge. He was killed in the combat shortly thereafter. West Virginia University.

3

Hunter's Raid on Lynchburg

After capturing Staunton and linking with Crook, Hunter set out to fulfill the rest of Grant's plans. Grant wanted Hunter to cross the Blue Ridge and get to Gordonsville and destroy the vital junction of the Virginia Central and Orange and Alexandria Railroads there. Grant informed Hunter that Maj. Gen. Philip H. Sheridan's cavalry would be venturing forth from the Army of the Potomac toward the same destination. However, Lee had returned Breckinridge to the Valley, and the Kentuckian used his small force to block the gaps in the Blue Ridge Hunter needed to traverse to reach Gordonsville. With the gaps effectively obstructed, Hunter decided against moving on Gordonsville. Instead, he would continue southward in the Shenandoah Valley to Lexington and Buchanan. There, he turned east and crossed the Blue Ridge at Peaks of Otter and landed in front of Lynchburg, a vital logistics and railroad center for Robert E. Lee and the Army of Northern Virginia. If Lynchburg fell, Richmond and Petersburg would follow, and Virginia would become untenable. Hunter had undertaken a risky gamble, but if successful it might have proven decisive in Grant's fight against Lee. One of Hunter's staff officers noted that nothing less than a corps from the Army of Northern Virginia could save Lynchburg from Hunter. Ironically, Lee sent the Second Corps, Stonewall Jackson's former command, under the leadership of Lt. Gen. Jubal A. Early who prevented Lynchburg from falling into Hunter's grasp. Hunter then became the prey and retreated westward through the Roanoke Valley and into the mountains of West Virginia to avoid being cut off by Early in the Shenandoah Valley if Hunter's army attempted to head back to Winchester. The ensuing journey proved to be harrowing for the both man and beast with Hunter's army and earned the ire of Col. Thoburn.

*Major General David Hunter.
National Archives.*

June 10th: Staunton, Va. Orders this morning to move Southward via Greenville to Midway. Prisoners and wounded are being sent to the railroad via Beverly [WV]. We have no supply train yet. One was expected to meet us here.

June 10th: Midway, Va.⁶⁰ Left Staunton this A.M. at 7 o'clock - arrived here at 4 P.M. 18 miles. Gen'l Sullivan not being very well, I was placed in command of the Division. Crook's Division marched on a road west of us and camped tonight seven miles from here at Brownsburg. Genl. Averell's Cavalry passed east of us with the object of cutting the railroad between Charlottesville and Lynchburg. A train of over 200 wagons overtook us this evening.⁶¹

Jun. 12th: Lexington, Va. Left Midway yesterday morning and arrived here in the afternoon. The rebel Colonel [John] McCausland was here with a Brigade of Cavalry and Infantry. They burned the bridge over the river and gave us a few shots from the opposite bank as we approached. The commands of Crook and Averell arrived here with us. [Gen. Alfred] Duffie is not yet in – His cavalry is behind to the east of the Blue Ridge attempting to cut the Railroad between Charlottesville and Lynchburg. The country from Midway to here [Lexington] is not equal to that farther down the valley.⁶²

A large mail came up with the train [the] night before last, but no letter for me. I don't understand it. I have still regret the amount of pillaging and plundering that is taking place along the line of our march and around our camp. If there was nothing wrong in it itself, the destruction of discipline and order in the command would be enough to convince any good military man that the practice should be put down.

The Genl. Comd'g is burning the [Virginia] Military Institute and Arsenal at this place and also the private residence of ex-Gov. Letcher. The produce of the country is being brought in and when we leave there will be little left behind for the subsistence of the inhabitants. Plundering accompanies it all. We are to move this afternoon to the Lexington side of the river.

June 13th: Lexington Va. A detachment of the cavalry under Genl. Duffie that was went across the Blue Ridge to cut the Railroad has not yet been heard from. Some anxiety is felt concerning them. We remain at this place over today. The reports from Grant place him South of the James River. This comes from Rebel sources. Nothing definite is known of the whereabouts of the enemy in this direction. Rumor says that Gen'l Pickett's division is here or on its way.⁶³ Genl. Averell marched out last night with the intention of striking the Railroad South of us.

June 15th: Buchanan, Va. Left Lexington yesterday morning at 5 A.M. and arrived here at 7 1/2 P.M. 24 miles. Genl. Averell had preceded us and driven McCausland out of the place. He [McCausland] had destroyed the Bridge across the James River and from it several houses took fire and were destroyed, and the fire was prevented from extending to the other buildings by the efforts of Averell's men. Buchanan is a pretty little village with the Purgatory Mountains overshadowing it on the North and within two or three miles of the Blue Ridge on the east and southeast. The spurs of the last mountain range come down to the edge of town. On our march yesterday we passed within three miles of the Natural Bridge and were not able to turn aside to see it. Move this morning in the direction of Liberty.

Richmond papers of the 10th and 11th are rec'd. Their tone is hopeful and confident although they admit themselves to be in straightened circumstances. I can see no indications in them of any advantage gained by Grant within the present month. On our side gold is reported to be rising, being at the present time 194 per cent. This appears to be the crisis in the present war. The strength of the contestants is fully brought out on both aides. If the confederacy begins to go down nothing can save it. On the part of the U.S. it has the power to continue the contest and to continue it with greater energy than in the past. There may be a question as to their will to do so. Disaster now would bring such disaffection as followed the disasters to McClellan in 1862. But with our present resources failure must only result from the grossest mismanagement. I hope our army is different from the portion of it to which I belong. If I have any conception of right and wrong justice is on our side. But the issue is in the hands of a Power Who sees not as we see.

June 15th: Peaks of Otter. Left Buchanan yesterday morning. Passed over the Blue Ridge, road very bad; had been blockaded by the enemy. Went up on S. Knob last night to see the sunset - a magnificent outlook.

Move this morning at 5 o'clock. Enemy reported in force in the direction of Lynchburg. Genl. Hunter intends to press forward as rapidly as possible and attack before they are more heavily reinforced. We may have fighting before night.

4 P.M. On the road to Lynchburg, Va. Went into camp this P.M. on Otter Creek. Some cannonading is heard to the front. Averell has gone forward to cut the railroad east of Lynchburg. The enemy's whereabouts not positively known. Rumors put a considerable force between us and Lynchburg. Our men are not getting stores enough to subsist upon since we left Lexington.

We passed through the town of Liberty today. It is the county seat of Bedford County.[64] It is a beautiful little village. It has at present six hospital buildings full of wounded rebel soldiers containing, it is said, over 700 in all. The farm upon which we are camping was purchased last winter for $50 per acre in confederate money, which is about $3 per acre in Gold. It is a very good farm of 200 acres mostly under cultivation but has indifferent buildings upon it.

The people throughout the country here are in great fear of us. Many families leave their homes and run to the mountains. And many houses are left without an inhabitant when we approach. If the enemy is at Lynchburg or this side we will know it within the next 24 hours.

June 17th: Otter River. Left Otter Creek this A.M. at four o'clock. Are waiting here till a crossing is affected for the Artillery. Averell crossed yesterday afternoon and is now at New London, six miles to our front, where he is opposed by a force of the enemy that he is unable to drive way. Genl. Hunter does not believe there is any force that can materially retard our progress. Genl. Crook's command is marching towards Lynchburg on the R. R. destroying it as they go. The day will develop the enemy's ability to oppose us. Genl. Hunter must have good grounds for his confidence or he would not divide his force as he has done.

2 P.M. We are one-mile North of New London on the way to Lynchburg. Day excessively hot, men are disposed to straggle and fall out. All are on short rations. Our division gets no supplies whatever from the country since leaving Lexington.

Editor's Note: Jubal Early's troops began to arrive late in the day on June 17. Hunter's advance had driven the Confederate cavalry from its defensive positions just west of Lynchburg late in the day, but the opportunity to capture the city had slipped away. Most of Early's troops were still enroute that evening, so Early pulled off a ruse. One regiment of troops continually disembarked from a train, marched toward the front over a route visible to the Federals. All the while bands played and people cheered. Then the regiment stealthily marched back to the train station and board the train which departed a short distance out of Lynchburg before quickly returning with whistles blowing. The cheering picked up again, and the whole scene repeated itself during the night. Hunter heard the commotion and determined that the town was being reinforced significantly more than what was actually taking place. As such, his plan for the following day lacked aggression and seemed more designed to cover the withdrawal of his army from Lynchburg. Hunter launched some probing attacks on June 18, and Jubal Early responded in kind, but a general engagement did not develop.

June 19th: Two miles west of Liberty. Reached the enemy's works within three miles of Lynchburg on the afternoon of the 17th. The 2nd Brigade moved to the front and relieved a Brigade of the 1st Division about 9 P.M. Threw forward a Regt. as skirmishers and lay down under arms for the night. Skirmish firing continued during the entire night.

On the morning of the 18th the enemy was discovered within 800 yards of us behind strong earth works, which he was rapidly extending. Not less than 2,000 persons were busy with picks and shovels. Most of them were blacks. Our skirmish line was drawn in at daylight and during the forenoon we lay within easy rifle range of the enemy. Our lines being protected in ravines and depressions in the land. A fire from sharpshooters was kept up all the time. On the part of the enemy, [it] was very effective. Our Batteries were engaged with those of the enemy in feeling each other's position.

One Regt., the 18th Conn. was detached from my Brigade to support a battery on the extreme left of our line. Another the 4th W. Va. was sent in support of a battery on the right, and one regt. deployed as skirmishers on our front, leaving me three regiments in line of battle.

Towards the middle of the afternoon the enemy advanced upon us in force. Our line consisted of three regiments of Col. [George D.] Wells' Brigade and three of mine. As soon as the enemy advanced we met them with a shout and charge against which they immediately fell back and we pursued them to their earth works the first line of which was taken possession of. And one piece of artillery was captured. The enemy having a much stronger line of works in rear of the first and appearing to be in strong force our advanced line was moved back to its original position.

Several prisoners were also brought in and from them it was learned that several corps were in our front under command of Gen. Early. Other prisoners said that Early and Breckenridge's Divisions were all that had left Richmond. And acting on this information Gen. Hunter ordered the command to fall back, which was done last night. The command moved off quietly after dark and in good order reached Otter Creek where a halt was made and an issue of Beef was given to the troops. After which they moved to this place two miles west of Liberty.

Colonel George D. Wells.
Nick Picerno Collection.

June 22nd: Little Catawba Creek. Left Liberty at 1 1/2 A.M. June 20th, reached a point three miles east of Bonsack Station[65] at 2 P.M. Distance 18 miles. Enemy following close in our rear and occasional skirmishing. Moved again at 7 P.M. and arrived in Salem at 5 A.M. June 21st. distance eighteen miles. As the rear of the column neared Salem it was attacked by the enemy and for two hours rather vigorous skirmish firing was kept up with artillery and musketry.

The command, after four hours rest was put in motion in the direction of New Castle. Duffie's division of Cavalry took the lead. The wagon train and artillery followed. I was directed to accompany it with the Second Brigade as guard. Just as it was moving off with the wagon train, the order was countermanded, and I was directed to move back in the direction of Bonsack and attack the enemy who were pressing the rear guard.

The train was permitted to proceed without a guard. After going four or five miles it was attacked by a party not exceeding 200 in number, and two batteries were lost, and a panic got up with the train which might have lost us nearly the whole train if the rebels had only been prepared for their victory and followed it up with vigor. The attack upon the unguarded train was made in a narrow gorge on entering the spurs of the Catawba Mountains.[66]

We were detained until near evening removing obstructions from road in our front. At 6 P.M. moved across the Catawba Mountain and camped in the valley between it and North Mountain. Pillaging and wanton destruction of property has been on the increase during the last week.

I am making this note near a dwelling of an old, gray-haired man and his wife who were plundered first of everything eatable and then all the kitchen furniture was taken. The beds were stripped of all the bedding and everything about and in the house is broken down and destroyed. Crook's command is the worst at this kind of work of the infantry, but the cavalry is beyond them in their ability to do mischief throughout the country. I never could have believed until now that human depravity could get so low as to be guilty of the wicked atrocities that are committed on every side.

We have along with us a train of 600 wagons; over three hundred have already been sent home. These wagons are nearly all filled with plunder. Officers have their tobacco that they have stolen and are taking north to sell. They are also carrying away pictures, furniture, etc... Enlisted men, drivers and others are at the same business on a smaller scale. Woman's and children's clothes, chinaware and house furniture generally are picked up and stored in the train. But footsore, sick, tired, [and] wounded soldiers are left behind and in many cases are ordered out of the wagons that are carrying plunder.

The whole command is becoming more and more demoralized in consequence. But one case where anyone has been reproved for stealing has come to my knowledge, and that was the case of a poor follow who became infected with the stealing mania to such an extent that he laid hands on the horse of Genl. Hunter and appropriated it to his own use. The man was discovered and one hundred lashes were allowed to be laid upon his back. To steal from Gen. Hunter is a crime but to steal from a citizen of the country is not worthy of reproach.

June 21st: New Castle. 4 1/2 A.M. Arrived here last night [at] 11 o'clock. Command is in line and ready to start in the direction of Lewisburg. My Brigade is moving without breakfast. New Castle is the county seat of Craig Co. It is an insignificant village of about 30 families living in very humble dwellings. This country is mountainous and but poorly adapted to agriculture. The citizens say that there is a bed of Bituminous coal a few miles from here but little worked.

10 A.M. Barbour Creek. Halted for breakfast between Little Mountain and Seven Mile Mountain. Country rough. Marching slow, and difficult. The train moves slow and everything has to wait for it. No information from beyond. Don't expect to receive communications from within our lines for at least four days yet and maybe not then.

June 24th: Old Sweet Spring.[67] Arrived at this place last night at 10 1/2 o'clock. My Brigade came in in good order, having marched 23 miles and passed over three large mountains viz: Peters Mt., Middle Mt. and Little Mt. Probably not less than 500 horses gave out on the march and were left on the road. Sweet Spring is a pleasantly laid out place. Fine buildings full of good furniture. The water is rather pleasant than otherwise, and the sulphur in it cannot be detected. We move this afternoon for the White Sulphur Springs, 17 miles distant.

June 26th: Meadow Bluffs. Am sick with Dysentery. Have been riding in ambulance since yesterday morning. The whole command is out of rations. The men are starving. Have not yet commenced on mule or horse meat. Expect to meet supplies tomorrow.

June 27th: Big Sewell Mt. Am still riding in ambulance. The road is lined for miles with broken down and starving men who are sent forward in advance of the main body. The horses are staggering and falling down from exhaustion. No word from supplies but we expect to meet them this morning. The country this side of Lewisburg is rough and sparsely settled and poorly improved. The little supplies that were in it have all been gathered by Crook's command who went before us on the road and the poor inhabitants we find by the road side are famishing like ourselves. We talk of killing horse and mule for meat.

June 29th: Kanawha River. Day before yesterday we rec'd rations of crackers and coffee at Mannis Creek, two crackers to the man. A full ration had been sent us but it had been plundered by the starving division in front of us and less than half a ration remained. But it was no time for grumbling about short rations. I never saw men who rec'd food more gladly. Yesterday two full days' rations were forwarded to us, and the men are doing very well. Yet one month's time will not restore the vigor of health that was enjoyed before the raid began. To restore good discipline will require equally as long a time and to make good the evil we have done is simply impossible.

Today visited the top of the rocks called Hawk's Nest or Marshall's Pillars.[68] It is said to be 1,100 feet high and overlooks the rocky bed of New River, which runs almost beneath your feet. The scene is wild and attractive. The New River for miles back runs through narrow rocky gorges in the mountains. The Gauley River emerges from a similar channel and together they form the Kanawha, which in one mile from its rocky hearth tumbles over the Kanawha Falls, perhaps 15 feet. The country around is mountainous and broken.

Ate dinner today at Miss Hales, a country Hotel nearby. Had a good dinner and enjoyed it. We have gone into camp along the bank of the river, and the men are making good use of their time bathing and washing clothes. Rumors from Grant and Sherman are very favorable. Have seen no papers yet.

CHAPTER THREE   55

July 2nd: Kanawha Falls. Move this morning at 5 o'clock for Camp Piatt, there to take boats for the Delta for the Baltimore and Ohio Railroad. Rumors are that the rebs have occupied Martinsburg or some point in the neighborhood.[69]

3 P.M. Day warm and sultry. Nothing yet confirmed about an attack on the railroad. Paper of the 28th and 29th rec'd. News not important. Arrived at Camp Piatt 7 P.M. Boats are in waiting to take the command to Parkersburg.

July 3rd: Steamer "Lester McCombs." On the Kanawha River-low. Striking the bottom frequently. Day pleasant. Rec'd a mail with five letters from my wife dated from 1st to 21st of June.

July 5th: Ravenswood, W. Va. 8 A.M. The "Lester McCombs" ran aground one mile below here.

4

Back to the Valley: Chasing Jubal Early's Raiders

After Jubal Early forced Hunter to abandon his effort against Lynchburg, the Confederate commander followed the Union forces to the vicinity of modern Roanoke, Virginia. Once he was sure that Hunter had indeed retreated into the mountains of West Virginia, Early headed north down the Shenandoah Valley and invaded Maryland. Robert E. Lee himself had formulated this strategy to force Union commander U.S. Grant to detach troops from Petersburg to save Washington. Although Early had only 16,000 men in his command, Grant ultimately redirected two army corps to quell the Confederate raid. Early routed a Union force at the Battle of Monocacy on July 9 and demonstrated in front of Washington for two days, July 11-13, before retiring to Virginia on July 14. As Early noted, "We haven't taken Washington, but we've scared Abe Lincoln like hell." Meanwhile, Hunter's army retreated to Charleston, West Virginia, where they boarded riverboats on the Kanawha River. The plan was to ride the boats up the Kanawha to the Ohio River to Parkersburg, West Virginia, where the troops would take the Baltimore and Ohio Railroad to Martinsburg in the Shenandoah Valley. In theory, this would have placed Hunter in a prime position to block Early's retreat from Washington, but an extended drought in West Virginia lowered water levels and forced the army to disembark several times, adding two days to the journey.[70]

When Hunter's army arrived back in the Shenandoah, the War

Department instructed him to place his combat forces under the command of Gen. Crook, and assigned him to report to Maj. Gen. Horatio Wright who was pursuing cautiously Early from Washington. Crook marched from Harpers Ferry on July 15 in an uncoordinated attempt to disrupt Early's withdrawal. Even though it lacked synchronization with forces following Early from Washington, Crook's vanguard raided the center of Early's retreating column at Purcellville in Loudoun County, Virginia, on July 16, illustrating just how close the Federals had come to blocking the Confederate withdrawal. The delays in West Virginia had indeed been costly.

When Crook arrived to take command of his gathering troops near Hillsboro in Loudoun County, he found them woefully unprepared and promptly relieved Brig. Gen. Jeremiah Sullivan from command.[71] Crook promoted Thoburn to command Sullivan's infantry division and added an additional brigade that had previously served under Crook's command. Although Thoburn had once again received increased command responsibility, the commensurate promotion to brigadier general never came. What did occur was finding himself in a dire situation on more than one battlefield as the result of poor judgment by his superior officers.

During the transfer of Hunter's troops back to the active theater of operations, an acquaintance of Thoburn's from Wheeling encountered the 1st West Virginia along the B & O Railroad during a stop at the town of Piedmont, West Virginia, on July 6 or 7.[72] The campaign had worn hard on the men and tested the limits of their physical endurance, and the Wheeling resident barely recognized any of the men. The observer wrote, "Col. Thoburn, Lt. Col. [Jacob] Weddle and Major E.W. Stephens and other officers of the First were lying asleep in a freight car with dirty blankets for pillows. They wore 'the shadowed livery of the burnished sun' and looked rugged and healthy enough." He described them "as the roughest set of men he ever saw." They had not changed clothes for nearly forty days, "most of which time they had been on the march, over steep hills and through blinding dust, part of the time without food or water." And in this condition, Thoburn and his command went forth in the pursuit of Jubal Early.[73]

CHAPTER FOUR 59

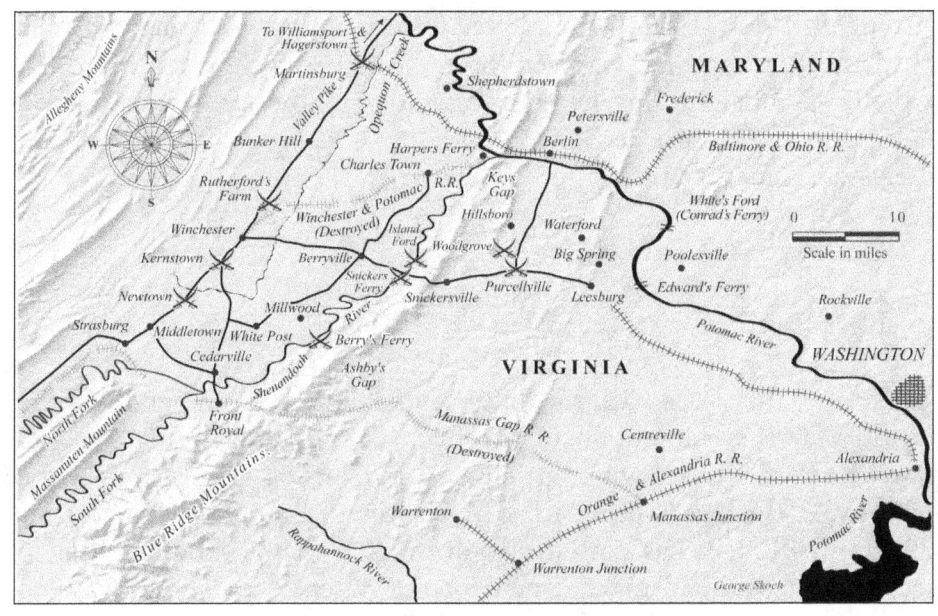

*Shenandoah Valley Campaign of 1864.
Area of Operations.*

July 8th: Green Spring River.[74] Arrived at this place last night. Have completed the South Branch Bridge - will move forward in a few minutes. Am here with my brigade on the cars. Col. Wells' Brigade is immediately behind me. The rebels are reported in force at Martinsburg.

7 P.M. Cherry Run.[75] Arrived here this P.M. No enemy in this immediate neighborhood. [Confederate Brig. Gen. John D.] Imboden is reported to have crossed at Williamsport this day. Nothing definite known about the whereabouts or number of the main body of the enemy. Genl. Jeremiah Sullivan has not yet come forward. In the meantime, I have command of his Division.

9 P.M. From the latest information, the enemy appears to be in strong force and inclined to move forward rather than fall back.

July 9, 1864. [Excerpt of a letter from Col. Joseph Thoburn to his brother, Thomas, who was serving in Sherman's Army during the Atlanta Campaign. This letter offers Colonel Thoburn's unvarnished opinions on Hunter's leadership and the Lynchburg Campaign and dreary assessments of the future.]

Cherry Run, B & O R.R.

Dear Brother:

I am at this place with the advance of Hunter's Command. We are waiting for the completion of the Back Creek Bridge. Then we will move forward. We know but little yet of numbers or whereabouts of the rebel force. They are believed to be in Maryland. Their movement in this direction will, if it has not already, overmatch that of Hunter's, and it results from the bad management of the latter. We went forward to Lynchburg too slowly, giving the enemy time to concentrated against us, and when we fell back, instead of returning down the valley keeping between the enemy and our base of supplies. We uncovered the R. R. and moved in a southwestern direction to Salem and home by the Kanawha, giving the enemy an open road to his present positions here, which he has at once taken advantage of.

I was never connected with anything that I so much disapproved of as Hunter's Raid. It was most disgraceful, sacking colleges, burning private dwellings, pillaging and plundering to an extent that could not be exceeded in the main feature that will make our expedition remarkable in the future. In our engagements with the enemy, we were successful, but we suffered more than we inflicted damage upon the enemy. My command lost 1,100 killed and wounded. This is a heavy proportion out of 3,000. But this includes Sigel's operations at New Market.

I am very much discouraged about our prospects, and I have my fears that our present management will never lead us to success. These fears I keep to myself. We are widening the breach between us and the rebels and making the Union more difficult.

Grant must be easily held for so large a force could not be spared from Lee to come in this direction. Ewell's who corps is thought to be here...[76]

July 10th: Cherry Run, B & O R.R. Move forward this morning to Hedgesville.[77] The enemy is still in Md. But small parties this side of the river. Very little positive information is rec'd concerning them.

July 11th: Martinsburg. Arrived at this place this A.M. at 10 o'clock. Two hundred and fifty soldiers of Vaughn's Brigade were here but retired in the direction of Winchester.[78] A force of 3,000 or 4,000 is reported at the latter place. The Secessionists here have a rumor that Early, who commanded the force that went into Md. has retreated in the direction of Leesburg. I came in with the 1st, 12th, and 4th W. Va., 2nd Md. Potomac Home Brigade and 2nd Md. Eastern Shore. Genl. Sullivan is expected here this evening with the 1st Brigade and one Battery.

11 A.M. A report, apparently reliable is rec'd to the effect that Early is marching on the Frederick Pike in the direction of Baltimore. Genl. Sigel has been relieved by Genl. [Albion P.] Howe, and the latter has been ordered from Harpers Ferry to Washington.[79]

Our military situation is by no means flattering. A call for another 300,000 men has been or is about to be made. The men are needed now and needed badly. Col. [Robert M.] Richardson commanding the 15th New York Cavalry is a drunken worthless officer and his cavalry are of but little use to me.[80]

5 P.M. Genl. Sullivan has arrived and placed Col. Richardson under arrest and sent him to Cumberland. No further information from the enemy.

July 12th: Martinsburg, W. Va. News today rather unfavorable. Enemy thought to be approaching Baltimore and Washington. [Gen. Lew] Wallace was defeated near Frederick.

July 13th: Orders to move to Harpers Ferry this P.M. at three o'clock. Genl. [Horatio G.] Wright is at Edward's Ferry with the 6th Corps. Another Corps from Grant's army is landing at Annapolis.[81] I fear that Grant will have to suspend his operations against Petersburg. Imboden is reported to be at Winchester, also a detachment from Vaughn's Brigade. Communications are cut between Baltimore and the

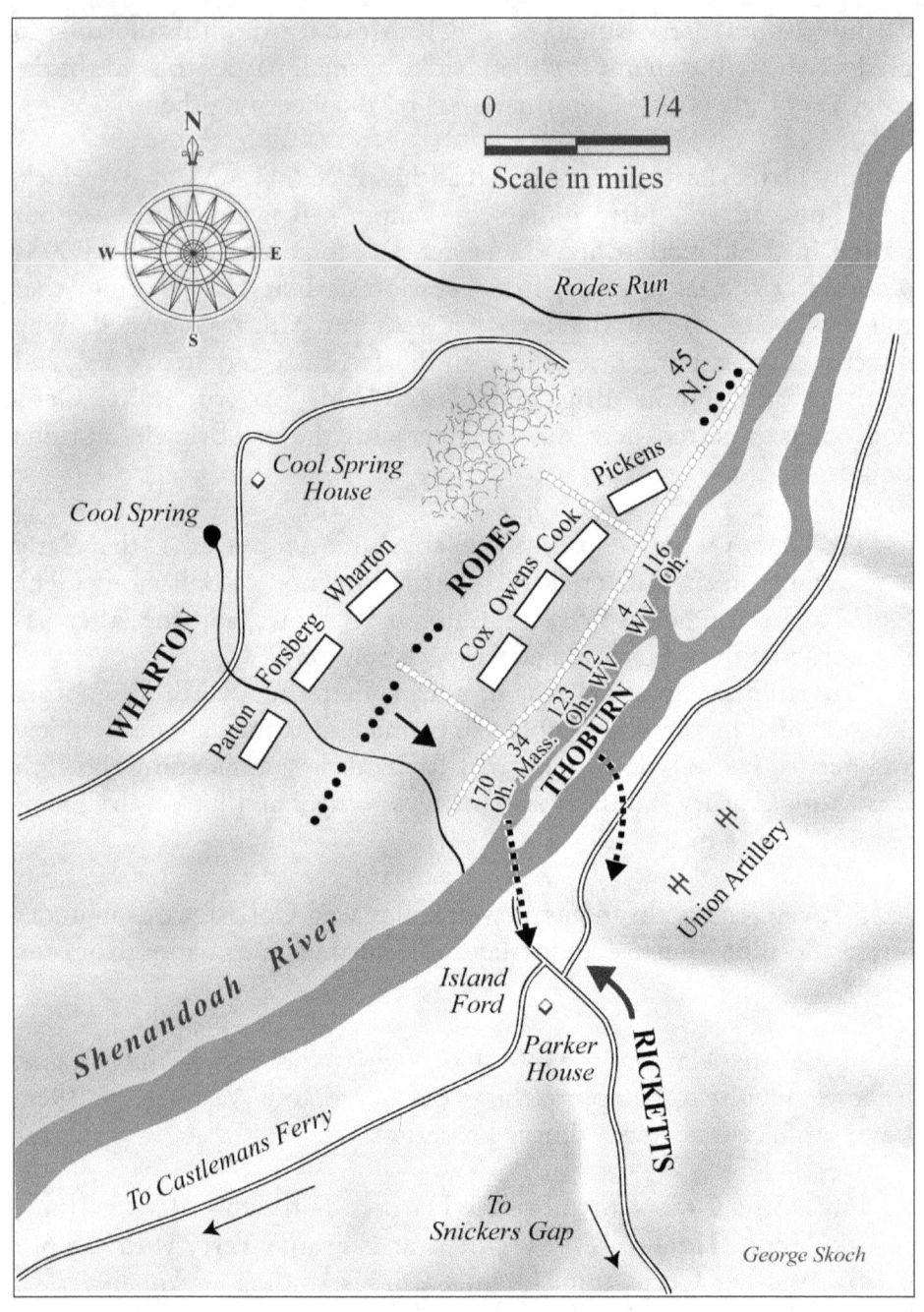

Battle of Cool Spring, July 17-18, 1864.
(Snickers Ford, Ferry, or Gap, as well as Island Ford or Castleman's Ferry).

North. Nothing heard from there since day before yesterday. Scouting parties are daily bringing in small squads of rebel soldiers. They are roaming about plundering all over the country.

July 14th: On the march to Harpers Ferry. Left Martinsburg yesterday at 3 P.M. marched to three miles beyond Kearneysville and camped for the night. Move this A.M. at 8 o'clock, Genl. Sullivan went on last night to the Ferry to take command of the force at that place. Maj. Genls. Sigel and [Julius] Stahel left the same point last night for Martinsburg. Sigel to take command there for a much smaller force thus the greater (in rank) gives place to the less. But in all our changes it is one mediocre for another. Our cause suffers for lack of a man of commanding talents who can bring success.

July 14th: Weverton, Md.[82] 7 P.M. Arrived here at 12 M, having marched 25 miles from Martinsburg, the enemy are reported crossing the river 20 miles below here. I know not whether we will be marched in pursuit.

July 15 P.M. Orders to move this morning. A command of dismounted cavalry is attached to my brigade under command of Col. Samuel B. M. Young, numbering 1,250 men.[83] Dr. David Baguley [1st West Virginia] has been dismissed from the U.S. service for making a very discouraging report concerning the condition of our men. It is expected that his dismissal will be revoked as his statement was not an exaggeration of facts.[84]

2 P.M. Lovettsville, Loudon Co. Va. Some difficulty was experienced in crossing the Potomac. The attempt was first made at Weaverton but the river was too deep. We finally crossed near Berlin. The enemy is reported near Leesburg with pickets 3 miles this side. The day is warm, road very dusty. No rain has fallen here since the early part of May.

July 16th: Hillsborough, Va, Arrived here yesterday evening, Our bags have not yet arrived. No orders this morning to move, The enemy are quietly moving away through Leesburg, and we are apparently doing nothing to prevent them. T'is true our force is too small to oppose their entire army; still we could worry and impede their retreat until other

Cool Spring Battlefield.

*Shenandoah River crossing at Cool Spring.
The combat occurred on the bank to the left in the picture.*

forces would come up. This Department apparently moves without system. Yesterday morning we were ordered to cross the Potomac at Weverton. The command moved to the point where it was found that there was neither ford nor ferry to cross upon. We moved then three miles further down the river and found a ford where the infantry crossed but the artillery and train had to go back to Harpers Ferry and cross on a pontoon Bridge. They are not yet here. Had the proper staff-officers made the proper inquiries in time, we would have had everything here last night.

12 M. Genl. Crook has arrived and taken command of all the troops moving in this direction, Genl. Sullivan is relieved of his command and ordered to report to Genl. Hunter. A large force of the enemy is reported moving in this direction from Waterford. Col. Wells has moved his Brigade out in that direction. Cannonading has been heard in the direction of Leesburg.[85]

10 P.M. Purcellville, Va, Left Hillsborough this evening and arrived here about dusk. The rebel army is all past. Their rear passed about one hour before we arrived. I am pleased with Genl, Crook and like the change, but the change is not over yet. Our Division is yet without a Commander, and we may not fare so well when one is appointed. Probably the ranking Colonel will be put in command. Col. Mulligan will in this case be the commander.[86] Am putting up at the house of Mr. Asa Janney a Staunch Union family.[87]

July 17th: Purcellville, Va. 8 A.M. Genl. Wright with the 6th Army corps is 4 miles from here in the direction of Leesburg. The rebel army has retreated through Snickers Gap. We are out of provisions and in poor condition to pursue, and but little is expected from our pursuit.

July 18th: Snickersville, Va. 12 M. Left Purcellville this A.M. at 4 o'clock. Have been here in the sun for three hours. Enemy reported to be through the Gap on the other side of the Shenandoah. Genl. Wright commanding 6th Corps has just come up. Col. Mulligan's brigade had a skirmish with the enemy in the Gap yesterday evening and was compelled to fall back.

July 19th: Snickers Gap, Va. Moved forward through the Gap yesterday about 1 P. M. I was put in command of Sullivan's old Division and the 3rd Brigade of Crook's, and was directed by Gen. Crook to proceed by a circuitous and hidden route to a fording, one and a half miles down the river and effect a crossing and up the other side and drive the enemy from the upper ford on the Berryville Road. The impression then was that the main body of the enemy had retreated leaving only a rear guard to dispute our passage of the river. On reaching the fording we found the enemy occupying the opposite bank with a strong picket of about 150 or 200 men. By making a rapid dash across the river the picket was driven away without loss to us. We captured a Capt. and eleven men. The captain was a staff officer on Gen. [Armistead] Long's staff.[88]

Lt. James H. Rider.
Thoburn's adjutant general was severely wounded
at the Battle of Cool Spring, July 18, 1864.
Photo courtesy of Richard A. Wolfe.

From the prisoners, information was gained that 2 divisions of Early's army were within one mile of the ford and the remainder of the command not farther than 4 miles distant. This news was sent back to Genl. Crook and a position was taken near the river bank and a strong skirmish line was sent forward about half a mile. A line of rebel skirmishers surrounded ours a half mile farther out. In this manner we lay for about one hour when their skirmish line advanced in very heavy force and our line fell back. Behind their skirmish line, a heavy column advanced upon our right flank.

About one thousand of the dismounted Cavalry broke and ran across the river. A panic was created by this and a great portion of several regiments followed them in wild disorder. A portion of the line towards the right was entirely deserted and for a short time we were on the verge of disaster. But two regiments [116th and 123rd Ohio] from the left were double-quicked to the right and the enemy were checked and finally driven back.[89] Two other attempts were made to dislodge us, but both were repulsed. About dusk I rec'd. orders to recross the river which was done in good order. Our loss was comparatively light considering the character of the contest which was very stubborn and determined. The men were protected by the embankment of a road that ran along the river bank and under a large bluff. The total killed and wounded will not exceed perhaps 200.[90] The loss of the enemy is much greater, probably three times as much. We are resting today very quietly. The 6th Army Corps and a portion of the 19th is here. No attempt is being made to cross again to the other side of the river. What the enemy is doing, we know not. The way is open for him to again destroy the railroad at Martinsburg. If they are disposed to do this it will not be difficult to accomplish for our force at that place and Harpers Terry is not large. Genl. Crook has added the 3rd Brigade of his old Division to Sullivan's Division and has given me command of the whole. This arrangement will probably not last longer than the present pursuit of the rebels for after that Genl. Crook may be returned to the Kanawha with his old command.

July 20th: 5 A.M. Orders were issued last night to be ready to move at a moment's notice and an hour afterward countermanded. The intention was to move to a lower ford on the river near Halltown. Information was received that Hunter was occupying Charlestown from which place he had driven the rebels. We heard cannonading that direction in the forenoon.⁹¹ About sunset last [evening] cannonading was heard in the direction of Ashby's Gap, whither our cavalry are said to be.⁹²

Lt. James H. Rider, my Adjutant Genl. was severely wounded in the right arm during the engagement day before yesterday; also Sgt. Stockton Carmack an orderly who had been with me as such for over two years. Col. Daniel Frost of the 11th W.Va. was mortally wounded and died last night. Col. Washburn of the 116th Ohio has a dangerous wound in the head. Lt. Col. Thomas Morris of the 15th W. Va. was mortally wounded and left on the field. Lt. Col. Edward Murray of the 5th N.Y. Heavy Artillery was killed. The loss in officers was proportionally heavy and was far out of proportion to the number of enlisted men killed or wounded.⁹³

Capt. George W. Hoge of the 126th Ohio is here with the 6th Corps.⁹⁴ He does not believe that the Army of the Potomac will accomplish much before the close of the present season. He puts the loss in killed and wounded since crossing the Rapidan at 50,000. He says digging is all the rage in both armies, that whenever a movement is made the first thing done on going into a camp is to entrench, and that either army well entrenched cannot be driven away without great loss. That this is so apparent to both sides that comparatively few attacks will hereafter be made or at least few attacks are now being made. From Capt. Hoge, I get some news from home; my brother David is nominated by the Union Party as a candidate for Auditor of Belmont County. I do not expect him to be elected as the county is strongly Democratic and will give an opposition vote. Unless some very brilliant success will attend our arms, the Democratic Party will very likely carry the fall elections.

10 A.M. The whole command is moving across the river. The enemy having disappeared from the opposite side. 5 P.M. Moved across the river and went into camp. Enemy reported to be moving off in the direction of Strasburg. The citizens report heavy losses to the enemy in the engagement day before yesterday. A rebel surgeon left in charge of the wounded states their loss at 60 killed and 380 wounded. Our loss in killed, wounded and missing will not exceed 300. Crook says that we will remain here for two or three days, our men need it [rest].

CHAPTER FOUR 69

Col. Daniel Frost, 11th West Virginia, was mortally wounded leading a brigade under Thoburn at the Battle of Cool Spring on July 18, 1864. Nick Picerno Collection.

5

The Second Battle of Kernstown and Another Retreat

When Early withdrew from the area near Snickers Gap, Maj. Gen. Horatio Wright concluded that "the object of the expedition had been accomplished" and rapidly led the Sixth and Nineteenth Army Corps, nearly 20,000 men, back to Washington and leaving Maj. Gen. George Crook's little Army of West Virginia to conduct operations in the Shenandoah Valley on its own. Lt. Gen. Jubal A. Early's force numbered approximately 16,000 men at this time with the vaunted Second Corps of the Army of Northern Virginia (Stonewall Jackson's former command) forming the nucleus of the Confederate Army of the Valley District. Crook mustered only 14,000 troops against Early's army, and those troops lacked the combat experience possessed by most of the Southern veterans. Crook recognized Early's advantage. Crook incorrectly believed that Early had detached "a good portion" of his army from the Valley under orders from General Robert E. Lee to return to Richmond. Even so, Crook realized that his "only hope" was for Early to divide his command. In reality, Early's entire army had only fallen back to Fisher's Hill, a little more than twenty miles south of Crook's position at Winchester. Early and his force remained a credible threat to the Union cause in the Shenandoah Valley and was poised to strike when the opportunity arose.[95]

General Lee had been pleased with the results of Early's operations in the Shenandoah Valley; he had siphoned the Sixth and Nineteenth

Corps under Maj. Gen. Horatio Wright from Grant's operations against Richmond and Petersburg and in doing so very likely allowed Lee to survive Grant's repeated operations. Lee desired that the troops that Grant had detached to secure Washington remain in the Valley instead of returning to Grant against the Army of Northern Virginia on the Richmond and Petersburg front. As such, Lee informed Early that he could remain in the Shenandoah Valley if his operations assured that Wright's troops did not return to Petersburg. Early learned from prisoners captured in a cavalry engagement on July 23, that Wright had marched back to Washington. Seeking to carry out Lee's wishes, "Old Jube" went on the offensive on July 24 and inflicted one of the most embarrassing defeats ever suffered by the Union cause in the Shenandoah Valley. Losing no more than 200 men, Early inflicted 1,200 casualties on Crook's army in a tactically brilliant attack against the Federals. Once again, Col. Joseph Thoburn found himself in a defeat that was largely the result of his commander failing to react to accurate warnings of the presence of Early's entire army in the Valley.[96]

At Second Kernstown, Thoburn's division was on the far right or western flank, and largely avoided the chaos and confusion that befell the left and center. Crook quickly realized his predicament and ordered Thoburn to Winchester where he served as the rear guard, deploying his troops in old earthworks that had been constructed by Maj. Gen. Robert Milroy's army in 1863. Covering the rear during a night time retreat with much of the army in confusion, Thoburn experienced several close calls and ultimately escaped by a roundabout route that separated him from the army for several days.

July 22nd: Castleman's Ferry. 5 P.M. The command moved this A.M. at 6 o'clock on the Winchester Pike. Gen'l. Crooks name this morning is signed Maj. Genl. I suppose he has been promoted. The fording at which we fought on the 18th is called Parker's Ford, sometimes it is called Castleman's Ford. The enemy's loss is reported to have been upwards, of 80 killed and 500 wounded. Gen. Breckinridge was immediate command and Genl. Rhodes' (sic) Division was engaged against us.[97] Three of their Cols. are reported to have been killed. Our information of the enemy's losses is received from our wounded and also from the citizens who are generally of rebel proclivities and will not exaggerate to their disadvantage.⁹⁸ The command is longing for a mail. I have not had a letter from my family since the 19th of last month.

There is a feeling beginning to pervade the command that our military affairs are not in a satisfactory situation. I fear we will have no success until radical changes are made in our policy. The vindictive spirit that is manifested towards the people of the South may be just but it is not calculated to win them back to Union and fraternity with us. On the contrary they are maddened and made desperate in rebellion. Justice must be tempered with mercy. When the whole people are in rebellion they must be conciliated. The Government should be mild and forgiving as well as firm and true to its own integrity. If a change of policy in this direction is not soon made, our cause is hopeless and the Union will be finally dissolved.

Brevet Major General George Crook. National Archives.

July 23rd: Winchester, Va. 10 A.M. The command arrived at this place yesterday afternoon. Here we met the remainder of Genl. Crook's command and Genl. Averell.⁹⁹ Our advance on the Strasburg road was driven in last night and the enemy pressed in our pickets this morning about 6 o'clock. The whole command was immediately marched to the front and put in line of battle. Until this time, no demonstration in force has been made against us though small skirmishing parties are firing upon our front and flanks. Genl. Crook issued an order dividing his infantry into 3 Divisions of two brigades each. I command the first composed of Sullivan's command. Col. Isaac H. Duval commands the 2nd and Col. James A. Mulligan the 3rd. A Baltimore paper of yesterday was read this morning. This is fresh news but there is not much to it. The accounts from Sherman before Atlanta are favorable.¹⁰⁰ Some informal

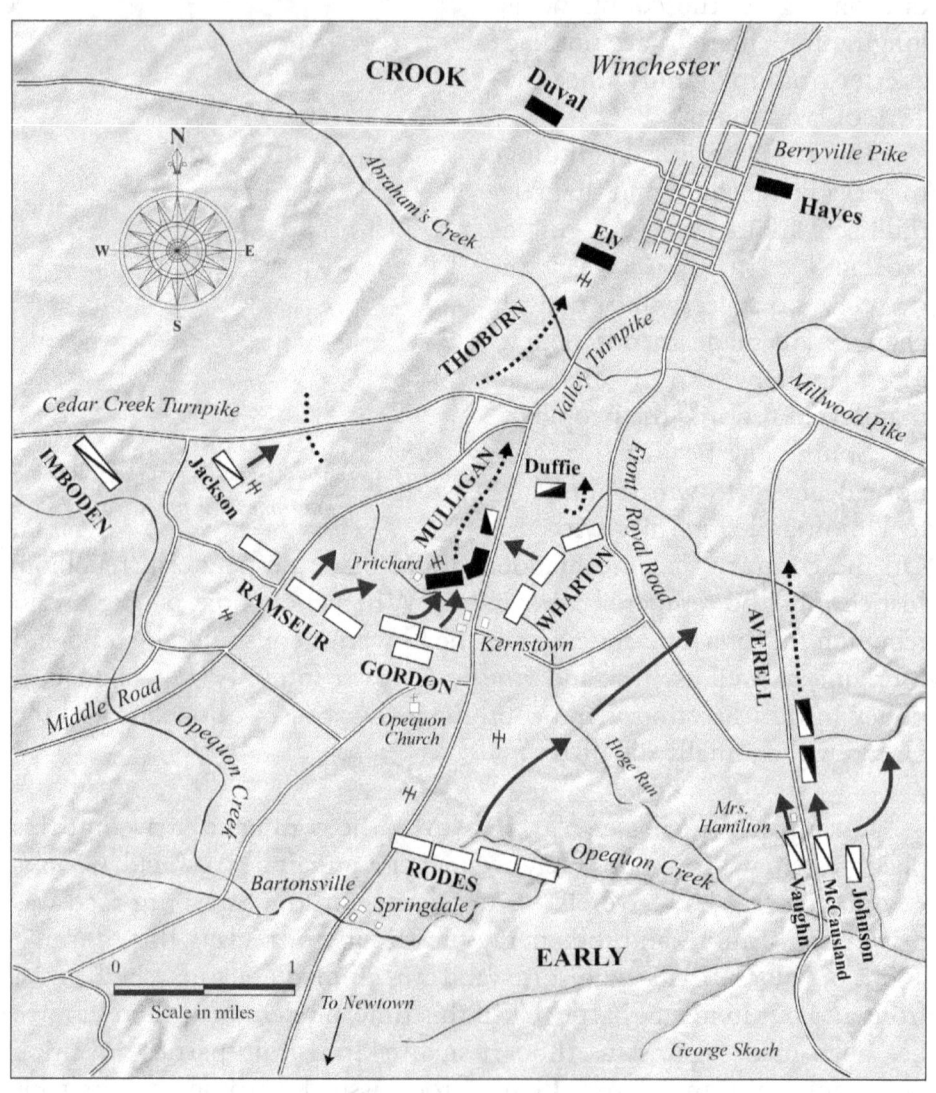

Second Battle of Kernstown, July 24, 1864.

negotiations looking toward peace have been going on between some ostracized rebels in Canada and Horace Greely. But no consequence is attached to it as the parties are not authorized to act for their Governments.

6 P.M. The enemy have retired from our front without offering battle. Their Cavalry had a skirmish with our cavalry in which we got the worst of it losing about 20 men. The enemy's force is not supposed to be large.

July 24th: This morning our pickets were driven in about 6 o'clock. The troops were all marched to the front. My Division was assigned to the right. For four hours nothing but slight skirmishing was attempted by the enemy, but his demonstrations were on a more extended scale and evinced a determination to make a more earnest stand than the day previous. I had my division strongly posted in a wood on the extreme right our front and flank strongly protected by barricades of rails, logs, etc. (this had been done the day before).

10 A.M. I sent the 2nd Brigade to Genl. Crook to be posted in front of his batteries at the center and ordered Col. Wells with the 1st Brigade to advance through a long wood (past the scene of Shield's Battle) on the right & turn the enemy's left flank. I with 2nd Brigade was directed to attack in front at the time he struck them on the right. But ere Col. Wells had advanced through the wood, evidence was obtained that the enemy were massed in his front in heavy force. I was ordered to move the 2nd Brigade to the right and with the two, attack. During this time, the left wing under command of Col. Mulligan was attacked and being pressed back.[101]

Genl. Crook saw that the enemy heavily outnumbered us and at once gave orders to retire. My skirmish line had been for some time hotly engaged and were suffering severely from the enemy's sharpshooters (who are supplied with a much better arm, and also ammunition, than ours. In fact a corps of trained sharp shooters is not known to us).[102] My division fell back in perfect order though annoyed by the enemy's fire. I took position on the hill south of Winchester and held it until the rest of the command were north of Winchester. My skirmish line alone being engaged. Col. Wells Brigade was sent to

Martinsburg with the train. Col. [William G.] Ely's [Second] Brigade alone covered the rear and retired by the north of town without the slightest confusion, being all the time annoyed by the enemy's sharpshooters from the gardens and out buildings of the town. As we fell back, we found Col. [Isaac H.] Duval with a Brigade on our right and the enemy in attempting to get on that flank met with unexpected volley from behind a stone fence [from Duval's troops] that made them fall back in confusion.

When I reached the fort south of Winchester everything was in full retreat. I directed Col. Ely to form a line of 2 regiments and 500 or 600 yards behind that another line and a third line a like distance still to the rear. When the first line delivered its fire it was to fall back in rear of the third line and again take position, and so on with each line. About the time this movement was commencing, my horse Charlie was struck with a cannon ball on the rump passing through under the saddle and coming out at the side of his neck. The back of my coat and hat were splattered with his blood and flesh. I have always avoided taking him under fire. I was much attached to him. After leaving Winchester, the right was not much disturbed by the enemy, except skirmishing and occasional shots from artillery. I had the fragments of Col. Mulligan's division gathered up and attached to the 2nd Brigade and also formed a junction with Col. Duval's Brigade, making altogether a formidable command. The enemy pressed the force on the right of the pike (east) which fell back rapidly leaving us on the west in rear of the enemy.

We marched along keeping one quarter of a mile off the pike until after dark when under the direction of a citizen guide that I had pressed into service, we were marching through a wood to get on the pike near Bunker Hill. On emerging from the wood, I discovered not more than 150 of the command following me. The remainder of the command had become in some manner separated from us. Supposing it to be but a few hundred yards back in the woods, I started the advance on the pike and went back with Col. William B. Curtis of the 12th W. Va, to bring forward the command. But on entering the wood, I could hear or see nothing of it. I rode back and forth in the darkness, finding it hopelessly lost from me or myself unable to find it. I started back to join the advance, but had gone but a few rods when I ran into some rebel cavalry and had to dismount and jump into a corn field in order to escape. Col. Curtis went [with me] and made good his escape, taking with us pistols and swords. We started as we thought to strike the pike north of Bunker Hill, but after going some miles we waked a citizen and found that we were going back towards Winchester. We immediately retraced our steps and as day was beginning to dawn we came up to some troops, concealed ourselves in some black berry bushes, and waited for daylight in order to ascertain whether we were with friends or foe. Cannonading opened after daylight and we found ourselves lying in rear of the rebel army, with them between us and our army.

We could not move without being discovered. A heavy rain had set in set in. Drenched with rain, cold, hungry, and thirsty (we had eaten nothing since the morning before), we lay shivering on the ground until 3 o'clock in the afternoon. When quiet prevailed around us, the enemy having advanced towards Martinsburg, we emerged from our hiding place and made for the North Mountain dodging along fences and through woods. We arrived at the foot of the mountain about sunset and were fortunate in finding a Negro cabin where we received a friendly greeting and a good supper of bread and milk which we highly relished. From the Negroes we learned that the rebels had a strong picket on top of the mountain with a signal station and also a patrol on the road to Ganotown in Back Creek Valley.[103] We crossed the mountain keeping the road to our right, crossed Back Creek near Ganotown and passing west of that town, made down the Back Creek Valley. About day light, we waked up a farmer and found ourselves within one mile of Shanghai.[104] We got our breakfast and took a short nap. The first either of us had slept since the night before the battle. We were both very nearly broken down. I had slightly sprained one of my legs in falling from my horse and had walked about as far as I was able to go. From this point down to the Rail Road the inhabitants were all or nearly all Union and intensely so. We procured horses and were conveyed by one farmer by back paths through woods and mountains to another who would take us a little farther. We reached Cherry Run the morning of the 27th but found some rebels there and had to fall back and go up to Sleepy Creek where we met a company of our own men, and also Capt. Peter B. Petrie in his famous Iron Clad. I got him to run us down the Railroad to Cherry Run when we found the rebels had left.[105]

We immediately crossed the river, reached the pike, took a hack and got to Hagerstown about dusk. Here I met Genl. William W. Averell who embraced me as if I had been his own brother returning from the grave.[106] Stayed all night in Hagerstown and reached my command on the afternoon of the 28th at Sandy Hook [near Harpers Ferry] and was gratified with a hearty welcome from every one. My division was in much better shape than I expected. Col. Mulligan's Division was consolidated into a Brigade and given to me making my division number over 6,000. Col. Mulligan and Lt. James Nugent were killed on the battle field at Winchester. Col. M. was a brave, high-minded, and honorable man, brilliant in conversation, and in thought perhaps more ideal than practical. He was perhaps more popular outside of the army than in it.

Col. William B. Curtis commanded the 12th West Virginia and served under Thoburn throughout the 1864 Shenandoah Valley Campaign. Curtis's regiment rendered exceptionally good service at the Battle of Piedmont on June 5 and Snickers Gap on July 18.
West Virginia University.

6

A Change of Command

General George Crook's defeat at the Second Battle of Kernstown and his subsequent withdrawal toward Frederick, Maryland, north of the Potomac River allowed the Rebel Lt. Gen. Jubal A. Early to advance his cavalry into Pennsylvania where they burned Chambersburg, Pennsylvania, to the ground on July 30. Capt. Achilles Tynes of the 14th Virginia Cavalry described it as the "saddest spectacle that I ever witnessed to see the women and children." This event sent shockwaves through the Lincoln Administration, coming as it did only eighteen days after Early's army had arrived at the very gates of Washington, D.C. Coupled with Grant's embarrassing defeat at the Battle of the Crater on the same day as the Chambersburg conflagration, the prospects of victory for the north did not appear imminent to the administration and the northern electorate. Changes were needed and Grant would have to ensure that no further embarrassing episodes originated out of the Shenandoah Valley.[107]

As the *New York Times* explained, "the same old story over again, the back door, by way of the Shenandoah Valley, has been left invitingly open." Grant and Halleck had actually exchanged correspondence on strategy for the Valley even as the battle raged on the fields of Kernstown on July 24. Grant informed Halleck, the U.S. Army's Chief of Staff, that he preferred "a complete smash-up of the enemy's [rail] roads about Gordonsville and Charlottesville to having the same force

[Wright's] here [at Petersburg]. Even before they learned of Crook's defeat, Halleck suspended the return of Wright's Sixth and Nineteenth Corps to Grant.[108]

Meanwhile, Grant consolidated several commands into one to ensure unity of command against Confederate operations along the Potomac and in the Shenandoah. He initially placed the newly formed Middle Military Division under Maj. Gen. David Hunter with Maj. Gen. Philip Henry Sheridan taking command of the army in the field. Hunter recognized the cumbersome nature of the arrangement and submitted his resignation. Grant praised Hunter's patriotism at his willingness to stand aside for the good of the service. The future of the campaign and much of Lincoln's hopes for reelection now rested in the untried hands of Sheridan. For Thoburn, this period provided a brief respite from the hard marching and fighting that had characterized most of the spring and summer thus far. It was a time where hope waned and final victory seemed elusive, even for Abraham Lincoln who doubted that he would be reelected in the coming November elections.

July 31st: Middletown, Md. 9 A.M. On the evening of the 28th moved across the Potomac River to Halltown. The same evening, the 6th and 19th corps arrived. Yesterday information was rec'd that the rebels were crossing into Maryland above Shepherdstown. We at once rec'd orders to cross into Maryland. Moved past Sandy Hook as far as Burkittsville and went into camp. Afternoon: very hot. Many of the men fell down with sun-stroke and scarcely one-half of Crook's command marched into camp. Started this morning at 5 o'clock. At foot of South Mountain, 5 P.M. 2 miles from Wolftown. The day has been excessively hot, road full of stragglers, large numbers reported to have fallen with sun stroke. Rumors of the whereabouts of the rebels conflicting. Some say they have recrossed into Virginia. Others that they have gone into Pennsylvania. We have marched through fine country passed through the villages of Knoxville, Petersville, Middletown and Belleville. The people everywhere manifest a great friendship towards us.

I procured a very fine horse from Capt. Robert S. Gardner[109] [Quartermaster at Harpers Ferry] yesterday in lieu of "Charlie" killed at Winchester. I have used up and lost more horses since Hunter's raid

Captain Robert S. Gardner was a quartermaster who had originally served in the 23rd Ohio Infantry but was transferred to the U.S. Volunteers Quartermaster's Department in 1862. Steve Cunningham Collection.

commenced than I did in the three years preceding, having had four [horses] shot, one captured and one die of disease. This summer's campaign has exceeded in severity everything I have before endured.[110] This campaign is a more vigorous one everywhere; the contestants seem more in earnest. Such a conflict as we are now having cannot possibly endure long. Its severity must wear, cut, and exhaust the contestants. The Rebels cannot endure another summer's struggle like the present. So if we continue as we now are we must conquer, and peace will soon come. But there is a possibility that peace may soon come from another cause, the opposition party throughout the North is daily gaining strength and unless a series of victories will soon crown our efforts, they may carry the fall elections and elect a president favorable to peace or compromise, and foreign intervention in the form of mediation will with the incoming administration close the war. In either event this is the last year of the war, if these views be correct. I fear a premature peace that will leave slavery (the cause of our trouble) intact, will only postpone, not terminate our struggle. A peace on the basis of human and constitutional liberty will be permanent. Any other will be transitory.

The 6th and 19th Army corps have moved in the direction of Frederick City, the whereabouts of Averell is not known. Somewhere I suppose between Hagerstown and Frederick. Genl. Duffie is in our rear.

Aug. 1, 1864: Wolfsville, MD. 9 A.M. Started this A.M. about 8 o'clock marched but 2 miles when Genl. Crook rec'd information that caused him to halt and put the troops in camp for the day. Chambersburg has been burned by the enemy for refusing to contribute $100,000 that had been levied upon the place. Where they have gone from there is not known. A dispatch rec'd from Genl. Grant through Washington announces that on the 30th he exploded a mine under one of the forts at Petersburg and blew up the work. The 18th charged and captured the entire outer line of works. Our loss is said to be severe. Enemy's loss not stated. The prospect for taking Petersburg said to be good.[111]

Aug. 2nd: 10 A.M. The men are straggling over the country committing depredations upon the inhabitants [of Maryland]. I am doing all I can to prevent it but it still exists. This is the crying evil in our army. It results from a disregard private rights while we are in the enemy's country. No word is rec'd today from the enemy. From the fact that we are lying here idle, I suppose the enemy has withdrawn across the Potomac.

5 P.M. Orders received to move tomorrow morning for Frederick City. The enemy must be in Md. in earnest.

Aug. 3rd: Catoctin Mountain, 6 A.M. On the way to Frederick City. Yesterday's *Baltimore American* states that the rebels are retiring from Md. Also that Grant has been repulsed in his late attack upon Petersburg, and that our loss was severe. It will require fortitude on the part of our people to bear up under this disaster. The country has looked to Grant in his movement on Richmond and Petersburg as the big movement of the army. A failure with him is greater to bear than with any other army. The unfortunate Army of the Potomac is doomed to repulses. May the country bear them as well as the army does. Chambersburg has been burned by the rebels under McCausland. 3,000 of the population are left homeless and houseless. I hope retaliation will not be visited upon other towns in the south. Let the parties who fired the town suffer when they fall into our hands. It is thought by some that the Rebel Army under Early is marching through Loudon County, Va. on Washington.

The view from this mountain over the Middletown Valley and also eastward around beyond Frederick is very beautiful and imposing. Maryland in this region is equal to the best land I ever saw. If anything better than the best of the Shenandoah Valley. The price of good land here is from $75 to $100 per acre, i.e. before the war. Sent statement last night to ordnance office accounting for 86 packing boxes. Also statement to Adjt. Genls. Office accounting for non-rendition of monthly, return for November 1861; Issued Genl. order No. 2 against straggling, trespassing upon private property, etc... Hope to succeed the enforcing good discipline in the command. A thing much needed. My staff officers are intelligent and willing to discharge every duty. And zealous as well as willing.

Aug. 3rd: 2 miles south of Monocacy Junction, 4 P.M. Reached this point at 3 P.M., having marched 20 miles since 3 A.M. The 6th and 19th corps are here. No enemy to be heard of. All are wondering what we are brought here for. We are camped on the battle ground (on a portion of it) of Wallace and Early. Passed through Frederick, a beautiful town. Genl. Hunter has recently sent south some 40 families for giving aid and comfort to our southern enemies. All whom we saw upon the streets seem kind and friendly to the soldier and loyal to the Union. Visited the Hospital. Stockton Carmack is doing well. Has not yet received his furlough.

Aug. 4th: Monocacy River. From present indications we are to remain here in camp for a few days and get the men well fitted out and rested. After this our men will be fit for vigorous duty. My Division numbers about 5,000 aggregate present. 3,000 are absent-in Hospital and detached duty. One half of the latter number could be brought to the command in a week's time if the proper steps would only be made.

The policy of those in authority is such that commands are constantly getting lower and no efforts made to keep them up. Men are left behind for want or shoes and other causes. Under proper management, they could be fitted out and sent to their regiments in one week at farthest. As it is, months elapse before such men join us. Then again in ordinary marching and one day's work is sometimes so severe that the next is required to rest and recuperate the men. A simple minded farmer blessed with little common sense will hire men and work them in such a manner that they work steadily the whole year around. It is just as important that soldiers be treated the same way. And it is almost as easy to do it except on occasional cases when in rapid pursuit or in rapid retreat from the enemy. These occasions are comparatively few. Some intimations are dropped today from Genl. Hunter's Headquarters to the effect that Genl. Sullivan will again resume command of his old Division when his 4 days leave of absence is out. He belongs to the Dept. and if he claims duty at all there is only his old Division or Col. Duval's for him. His own he could claim being the larger division and his rank entitling him to it.[112]

Aug. 5th: Capt. Isaac A. Rosekrans, Commissary Bureau, U.S.A. reported this morning for duty relieving Lt. McIlwain who was acting as such. I regret this very much. McIlwain gave more satisfaction than the other will do. I will retain him on my staff as A.D.C. Capt's Angelo Crapo and Samuel S. Patterson of the U.S. Volunteers were assigned to my Division this A.M. and have been assigned to the 1st and 2nd Brigades as Commissaries of Subsistence for them. Col. Jacob Campbell commanding the 3rd Brigade has his command out today on drill. He is one of my best Brigade commanders. He is rough and uncouth but every inch a soldier. Col. George D. Wells commanding 1st Brigade is a very capable and intelligent officer but somewhat captious and irritable. Col. Ely commanding 2nd Brigade is milder and more genial than either of the others but lacks their energy. He is also hard of hearing which impairs his efficiency. Col Harris of the 10th W.Va. ranks Col. Ely but is in another Brigade (Col. Campbell's). He is a superior officer and I want him assigned to the command of the 2nd Brigade.[113]

9 P.M. This evening at half an hour before sunset, notice was rec'd that an execution would take place at sunset in presence of Crook's command. The doomed man was of the 23rd Ohio Volunteer Infantry. He had deserted to the enemy and was captured at Cloyd's Mountain. He escaped the guard and hired himself as a substitute and by a strange coincidence, very unexpected to himself, he was rec'd at the

headquarters of the 23rd last night among a lot of new recruits. He was at once recognized and tonight has met his fate. It is the first execution I ever witnessed. One year before the war, such a scene would be most exciting but at present when accustomed to the loss of life it is viewed with comparative calmness. Orders received to move immediately to the junction and take the cars for Harpers Ferry. Our two days rest is at an end. It has been a good rest for all. Orders countermanded. March to the Ferry starting tomorrow morning at 4 o'clock.

Information is recd. that the enemy in heavy force is crossing into Md. somewhere about or above Sharpsburg. The 6th Corps is moving down to the Ferry by railroad while Crook's command that has been marching has to go on foot. There is a prospect of a good deal of active field service in store for us for the next two months. Rumors are that reinforcements are on the way to us. The 2nd Army Corps is said to be on the way between this place and Washington.[114]

Col. Jacob M. Campbell.
Courtesy of Col. Jacob M. Campbell, Camp #14, Sons of Union Veterans.

Aug. 6th: On the way to Harpers Ferry. Genl. Grant was here last night in consultation with Genl. Hunter. Came after night and went away before morning, none knowing of his presence except those at headquarters. His presence here indicates some movements of importance about to take place in this direction. It is positively known that a rebel force is crossing the Potomac into Md. We were lying at Halltown with the 6th Corps when the word was first brought that the enemy was crossing into Md. We were all ordered to the neighborhood of Frederick City. The enemy did not cross at that time. Yesterday the report came that they were this time crossing the river, and at once we, marched back to Harpers Ferry. This, I suppose, is strategy. Common minds cannot see wisdom in it.

Harpers Ferry. 6:30 P.M. Just came in and went into camp in our old ground on Sandy Hook where I found the command when I came here from Winchester. Genl. Philip H. Sheridan is here and his cavalry are not far away it is said.

Aug. 7th: Sandy Hook. 7 A.M. A calm, pleasant Sabbath morning. Everything is calm and quiet and befitting the morning. But this seems more than a Sabbath calm. It is somewhat like the calm that precedes the storm. The enemy is thought to be in force in the neighborhood of the old Antietam battle ground. They are said to be fortifying the place and throwing up strong earthworks. 1 P.M. The 19th and 6th Corps are out in the direction of Charlestown, Va., the advance being in that place. We will follow soon.

~ End of Diary ~

CHAPTER SIX   87

Major General Philip H. Sheridan took command of the Army of the Shenandoah on August 7, 1864, which also marked the end of Thoburn's diary. Library of Congress.

Prologue

Sheridan's Valley Campaign

With the Burning of Chambersburg, Pennsylvania, Lt. Gen. U. S. Grant determined to make a change to the command structure that encompassed the Shenandoah Valley. He consolidated the districts that included the Valley, Maryland, West Virginia, Washington, D.C., and parts of Pennsylvania into the newly formed Middle Military Division. Initially, Grant retained Hunter in charge of the newly enlarged command and planned for Maj. Gen. Philip H. Sheridan from the Army of the Potomac to take command of the division's field army. Hunter resigned, believing that it would be better for the good of the service for one man to have complete control of the situation and that man was Sheridan.

On August 7, Col. Thoburn wrote his last entry into his journal, having filled it up. He wrote the following two letters to his wife and sent the "book," as he called it, home to his wife with these letters. He notes that he was starting a new journal, but that journal has not been located. Perhaps it was lost when Thoburn was mortally wounded in the early morning hours at the battle of Cedar Creek. It is unfortunate that we do not have his thoughts and views on the momentous campaign under the command of Maj. Gen. Philip H. Sheridan. That campaign saw several decisive Union victories that Col. Thoburn knew were necessary for the Union to prevail. While Thoburn's journal has ended, two letters to his wife offer some insight on his views of various commanders and his thoughts on the course of the war. His eagerness to return to his family is also revealed.

                              Sandy Hook.
                              Aug. 8, 1864

My dear Wife,

    I send you these sketches, most of them written by the wayside and a copy of what was in my mind at the time. It is far from complete record of the last two months. Many thrilling incidents are left untold, others only alluded to. To complete the History will require many winter evening stories from your tedious, talking husband, when in our own home, with our children around us, we will go over the past. But when I return to my family, I do not want to do much talking about myself. I hope I may not so far target myself as to become too gassy about what I've seen. This book is too big for my blouse pocket, and I send my old coat home so this note book may as well go with it.

    It is like myself; full of errors, but an indulgent wife will overlook them and judge them lightly. Do not judge my comments on the management of the war as favoring in the slightest degree the pretentions of the opposition party of the North. The Government must be sustained and the best peace is still be on the basis of Human liberty to all. Yet I have spoken of errors in the prosecution of the war that I can never approve of. General Hunter's army is no worse than others. Andrew and Thomas would tell you that Sherman's army acts as Hunter's did. The Army of the Potomac that we are now with behave as I have blamed Hunter's command for doing. I still maintain that this banditism and disregard for private rights of citizens who sympathize with our enemies is barbarous and unchristian. It is calculated to demoralize our own army and weaken its efficiency and also to estrange the people of the South more and more from us and make the restoration of the union more difficult.

    Hunter's raid if properly conducted would, in my opinion, have induced a large proportion of the inhabitants to look upon us with a more friendly eye than they had been doing; but instead of this, those who welcomed us will never want to see us again. Under such regime we can never bring back the South to the Union until we have trampled them in the dust beneath us, and this we will never do. I do not despair of ultimate success. I cannot see the end, but I believe it is not far distant. Heaven brings back an erring world to its allegiance by coming down to that world, being merciful to it, and returning it good for evil. A little of the same influence accompanying our present efforts would not be made in vain, and whilst I would hold out mercy and good will in one hand, with the other I would wield the sword with all the vigor I possess.

But I am one and a poor one. The nation is many and more wise than I. So I do not warrant my views as above theirs. I hope the next note book I fill and send to the family may wind up amid more peaceful scenes than this. The future can scarcely hold a time full of so much storm and strife. Good bye. May God bless you and the children.

Yours,
J. Thoburn

Bolivar Heights, Va.
August 9, 1864.

I expected yesterday to have sent this home with Mr. Hornbrook. He is here yet and will remain until tomorrow. Crook's command is now named the "Army of West Virginia". The whole command under [Maj. Gen. Philip H.] Sheridan is called the Middle Military Division. The whole command is lying in a triangle, the apex of which is Harpers Ferry. The Shenandoah and Potomac rivers are the sides and a line running through Halltown, the base of the triangle. General Crook's command is lying on the Shenandoah River. Today is a day of rest. Tomorrow we move forward perhaps to meet the enemy, at least we go forward prepared to do so. The trains are all left behind us until further orders. I do not know that it is definitely known what force is in our front. From the news in the Baltimore papers, one would suppose that we are going forth to meet the whole or nearly all of Lee's army, and from the quiet that reigns around us, one would suppose that no enemy was near us. Yet the rumor is that a line of rebel pickets surround us. The general impression is that the harvest in the valley is being threshed and taken away in the direction of Staunton. This is of great importance to them first, in subsisting their army, and second, in preventing us from subsisting ourselves in another such expedition as Hunter's.[115]

The army corps that came here from the Army of the Potomac are not so large as one would suppose. The 6th Army Corps does not number over 10,000 men. The 19th Army Corps from the Gulf is much larger. It is a mystery what becomes of all the men who are sent into the army. 700,000 were called out last winter and spring, at least 300,000 from previous calls should be remaining in the service. Still, there is not today 300,000 effective soldiers in the whole army. There are never as many sent out as the figures would imply and of those sent out a very large proportion are soon on the sick list or in Hospitals or on some detached duty that will relieve them from carrying the musket.

The great majority of the American people are not a fighting people to any very great extent at least. They have no reputation of getting up big armies and doing good fighting, but it is the few that lead forward and hold the many. Then it is a minority that has the courage to stand up when led forward. The great mass of the people would make any excuse to keep out of the army and out of danger. Large masses have volunteered but the majority of them have found some excuse or other to keep out of every engagement. A great deal of what passes for courage is pride. Many a man stands in danger trembling for his own safety while his pride will not let him run. Perhaps this should be called self-respect rather than pride. The men in the army who do the fighting have not, as a mass, that individual personal courage they should have, for they are subject to panics and confusion which should never exist among brave men. And at such times, the men who exhibit courage are few.

11 P.M. Information just received that Hunter has received a leave of absence to go to Washington, and that Crook is to take command in his absence, which I suppose means Crook supersedes Hunter. This will give satisfaction to the command and outside of it. But General Hunter is much more popular with his command than he was three weeks ago. His promptness in dismissing worthless officers has given satisfaction to good men. Under the structures of the press or from other causes his orders have been good.[116]

Good news from Mobile, if it does not turn out like the first news from Petersburg. No word from the enemy in our front. I don't wonder at your disgust about the papers, they have but little good news to give, and their correspondents are the companions of skulkers and stragglers, frequenters of good hotels and bar rooms. Newspapers are good things in times of peace, but not for war. I don't wonder at General Sherman banishing all correspondents from his army.

❧ ☙

Editor's Note: In the 1914 publication of this journal, Thoburn's letter to his wife ended at this point. But it continues in the actual journal and contains some frank opinions on Thoburn's commanders and his recommendations for a potential husband for his sister that offers a glimpse into Thoburn's thoughts on his staff.

❧ ☙

Dear Wife:

I will answer yours of the 3rd here and send with Mr. H. I would put my money into land as you suggest but I have no opportunity. Still there need be no hurry. First we will determine where we will buy and then make the selection and purchase.

Don't expect me home until late in the fall; the term of the regiment is out on the 14th of Nov. Some may be mustered out as early as the 5th of September when the enlistments for the regiment commenced. But I do not expect to be let off until the full term is up. I will not of course ask to be mustered out and will stay until there is no law to keep me any longer.

I don't wonder at your disgust about the papers, they have but little good news to give and their correspondents are they are the companions of skulkers and stragglers, [and they are] frequenters of good hotels and bar rooms. Newspapers are good things in times of peace but not for war. I don't wonder at Genl. Sherman's banishing all correspondents from his army.

Tell Mary to give my compliment to Mr. Dickey and threaten him with my vengeance if he proves an unworthy husband.[117] Tell her to be sure and invite me to the wedding. I'll come if possible. Tell Sis, I can't find her a few very worthy young man for her to select from.[118] But she must win them as well as choose. I have one man on my staff that is just the man for her, Captain George B. Macomber of Massachusetts.[119] He is strong and mild, brave and gentle, dignified and mindful. Educated and unassuming, talented and unpretending. And he is kind and tender and droll and quiet and reserved and c & c and furthermore he is just the man [with] light gray eyes. Hair and complexion like my own. A big head and very intellectual countenance.

Ask Sis how she likes him. He has good principles, never swears or drinks whiskey and is 25 years old. This is him to life. I could describe other young men but one is all she is entitled to. And if she won't take my pick, she need not look at the others. Lt. James H. Rider who was wounded is my favorite but he is not the man for Sis's husband for reasons not necessary to mention. Lt. Baker is a great big good hearted fellow, but Macomber is the man for Sis. Capt Isaac A. Rosekrans, my Commissary, is a fine fellow but he looks like a Dutchman that he is and is too slow for sis. Lt. Frederick Ballard is married and out of the question. Lt. McIlwain can't be beat, brave, bright, kind and gentle but hardly the man for Sis. Lt. Henry Hornbrook she knows. Lt. Brinniman, tall and slender, dark hair, and big, black mustache. Laughs and shows white teeth to a great extent; quick and active but not heavy enough for Sis. Dr. David Baguley is the last member of my family here. Maj. Herrick is absent sick and has too long a nose for Sis; when he is well and wants to know too much, and does know too much and makes too much use of what he knows to make a good husband. There, I have given Sis a view of my friends and is not Macomber the only man for her. Now tell Sis to be everlastingly grateful to me for such a man. I have given you as well as Sis a sketch of my staff, all good men and true, and all pleasant companions.

Captain George Macomber served on Thoburn's staff and was the man that he recommended as a potential suitor for one of his sisters.
Military Order of the Loyal Legion of the United States.

Your $20 is a small draw from the bank. I am spending just as little as I can help. On one page of this, you will find our worth in dollars and cents at the beginning of this month. Every month add a little to it. If I stay in the service till November, we may be worth $5,000 this is no more now than $2,000 was before the war. Still it is enough to get us a modest little home. If Providence spares us to get it. At the present low ebb of Gov't securities, our bonds could not be disposed of very well. The 5.20's sell now for 9 ½ percent premium. I never see the 10.40's quoted at anything and we [own] $1,300 of this stock. The $500 bank stock is worth its face at least. I have rec'd no pay since the 31st of March. Paymasters are waiting to come out and pay us whenever we are quiet enough for them to come safely. Expect to get paid before long.[120]

Gen'l. Hunter left for Washington this evening. His staff say he is not coming back to us. General Crook fills his place. I like the change. Crook is far the better man. He is a man of good moral character and I can trust him. Genl. Hunter reprimanded me for sending him a document that truthfully represented the demoralized and sickly condition of my command when he came home from his [Lynchburg] raid. I believe he did not like me and yet he had confidence in me, and often expressed it. And lately has spoken kindly of me in hearing of my friends. My relations with Genl. Crook have been very pleasant. He has trusted me with more responsibility after only a few weeks knowledge of me than any other commander has ever before done. And I am better pleased with him than any other commander I have ever had. This is not because I have been trusted by him, but for an earnest desire he always manifests to conscientiously perform his whole duty.

We move at 4:30 in the morning toward Berryville. Tis late, bed time, I must close. You may consider this book a good big letter if I don't write for some days. It will keep you going to read it. I will start another as soon as I get one. I wish it was better put together for you. Harvey's foot is well. He is in the tent with me (I have a tent now) fixing up my things. Henry Stock is in Frederick; so soon as he is able he will go home. I would get him promoted to a lieutenancy if I had it in my power. He merits it. A braver lad I never saw.

Good night and a good night's kiss – And may God bless you.
Faithfully yours,
J. Thoburn

Shortly after this, Sheridan's army advanced up the Valley in pursuit of Lt. Gen. Jubal Early's Confederates. Early made a stand at Fisher's Hill which resulted in a standoff between the two armies that ended when Sheridan learned Confederate reinforcements were heading to the Valley and began a week long withdrawal toward Harpers Ferry. During this time, a small incident occurred that displayed Thoburn's touch in dealing with his men that had earned him the regard and respect of his soldiers. A squad of soldiers from the 4th West Virginia Infantry had been out on the skirmish line all day until 11:00 p.m. near Cedar Creek. Earlier in the day, they had given a wounded comrade their only haversack containing all the whole squad's food rations. Upon being relieved from the line late at night, they returned to camp and searched for him in the darkness, calling out his name but failing to locate him. They passed an officer eating by the dim light of a lantern, and recognized him as Col. Thoburn, who called out, "Who are you hunting?" The tired and hungry soldiers explained their situation and lack of food. In his typical low-key manner, Thoburn replied, "Sit down here and eat your supper," sharing his hard tack, beef and coffee with the hungry soldiers.[121]

The Colonel continued in command of the First Division, Army of West Virginia, which was a part of Sheridan's 35,000-man Army of the Shenandoah. The West Virginian led his troops in Sheridan's abortive advance as far south in the Valley as Strasburg. When Grant informed Sheridan that Lt. Gen. Richard H. Anderson was joining Early via the Luray Valley, Sheridan pulled his army back to Halltown, four miles west of Harpers Ferry. As a result of the Union forces' repeated retreats to Harpers Ferry throughout the summer of 1864, Sheridan's army was dubbed the "Harper's Weekly." Sheridan and Grant had devised a plan to remain on the defensive and prevent Confederate commander Lt. Gen. Jubal Early from conducting further raids into Maryland and Pennsylvania. Only when Early returned his reinforcements to Robert E. Lee's Army of Northern Virginia would Sheridan attack. In the meantime, Sheridan's forces conducted daily raids and reconnaissance missions against Early's positions in the Shenandoah. Thoburn took part in several minor engagements that resulted from those actions.

On August 26, Thoburn's division participated in a severe engagement between Halltown and Charles Town. On September 3, Thoburn's division fought in the Battle of Berryville when Sheridan moved his army farther west as he jockeyed for position closer to the Confederate forces. Coincidentally, Confederate forces under Anderson were attempting to move eastward to pass through the Blue Ridge and operate in Loudoun County in an attempt to force Sheridan to divide his forces on both sides of the mountain. Instead, Anderson's advance under Maj. Gen. Joseph Kershaw of South Carolina ran into Thoburn's division as it bivouacked for the evening at Berryville. Kershaw overwhelmed Thoburn's advance, but Crook brought up the division of fellow Mountaineer Col. Isaac Hardin Duval and counterattacked. Duval succeeded in driving back the Southerners and restoring the Union battle line. Early came up to reinforce Anderson the next day, but finding Sheridan's position too strong to assail, the Confederates withdrew to their positions at Winchester.

For the next two weeks, the two armies faced off against each other across Opequon Creek. On September 15, Sheridan learned that Anderson had departed Winchester with Kershaw's division, and the Ohioan attacked Early on September 19, 1864. The ensuing action was the largest and bloodiest battle ever fought in the Shenandoah Valley. The Army of West Virginia spent the early part of the battle in reserve, while the two sides fought each other to a standstill after two hours of combat. With the Nineteenth Army Corps having been hit extremely hard on the Union right, Sheridan ordered Crook's Army of West Virginia into the fight to bolster that besieged corps. While Crook's men marched to the front, Sheridan rode over to the Nineteenth Corps and examined the situation in person. Its commander, Maj. Gen. William H. Emory, immediately expounded upon the brutal repulse his corps had experienced and exclaimed, "My dead are everywhere!" Unfazed by Emory's demeanor, Sheridan fired back, "You haven't begun to fight yet! I've got Crook here with 10,000 men, and I am going to throw them in and whip these fellows as they haven't been whipped lately." Sheridan followed through on his promise and more, adding two divisions of cavalry to the final offensive and sending the Confederates "whirling through Winchester," and earning the praise of President Abraham Lincoln. He wrote, "God bless you all, officers and men. Strongly inclined to come up and see you."[122]

Although the President did not visit the guerrilla infested war zone, the U.S. victory at Winchester was unprecedented and provided tremendous momentum to Lincoln's reelection effort. Never before had Union forces permanently routed Confederates from the Army of Northern Virginia from a battlefield in such decisive fashion. The Army of the Shenandoah lost 5,000 soldiers in the effort, while Early lost 4,000 and five pieces of artillery. Sheridan did not let up and pursued the Southerners the next day. On September 22, Sheridan attacked Jubal Early's forces again, this time at Fisher's Hill, a few miles south of Strasburg. There, Early had attempted to rally his army and make a stand on a range of hills that ran across the valley from the Shenandoah

Col. Isaac H. Duval served with Thoburn as the Major of the 1st West Virginia at the First Battle of Kernstown against Stonewall Jackson in 1862. By the time the 1864 Valley Campaign began, both men were commanding brigades and ended their military careers as colonels commanding divisions in Maj. Gen. Philip H. Sheridan's Army of the Shenandoah. Duval's active career ended when he was wounded at the Battle of Opequon Creek, or Third Winchester, on September 19, 1864. Military Order of the Loyal Legion of the United States Collection.

River west to Little North Mountain. It was a seemingly strong position, but Sheridan again relied upon Crook's Army of West Virginia to march along the side of Little North Mountain and attack Early's entrenched line on its left flank and rear. Thoburn and fellow division commander, Col. Rutherford B. Hayes, assisted Crook in convincing Sheridan of the merits of the flanking movement. The attack came off late in the day and routed the Confederates from Fisher's Hill, capturing 1,000 prisoners and as many as twenty guns by some accounts. Thoburn's official reports capture his role in these battles:

HDQRS. 1st INFANTRY DIV., ARMY OF WEST VIRGINIA,
September 30, 1864.

CAPTAIN: I submit the following report of the part performed by the First Infantry Division at the battle near Winchester on the 19th instant:

While lying at the Opequon about 12 m. of that day I received orders to leave my smallest brigade to guard the trains and move the balance of my command rapidly to the front on the Winchester pike, where the Sixth and Nineteenth Corps had been for some time warmly engaged with the enemy. I left Second Brigade and started at once with the First and Third. The pike was filled with wagons, artillery, ambulances, and stragglers running back from the scene of action, very seriously impeding my progress. After proceeding about two miles I reported in person to General Crook, and under his supervision formed my command in two lines on the right of the pike and in rear of a heavy wood, in the front of the which the Nineteenth Corps was posted and was at the time fighting the enemy.

The First Brigade, commanded by Colonel George D. Wells, of the Thirty-fourth Massachusetts Volunteer Infantry, composed the first line, and the Third Brigade, commanded by Colonel T. M. Harris, the second line. I then moved through the woods to the front, where I was directed to form on the right of the Nineteenth Corps, but on arriving at the front I found the right of this corps resting on a very deep and almost impassable morass, called, I believe, Red Bud Run, and having learned that Colonel Duval's division was to move up on the other side of it, I deemed it inexpedient to try to form my line as first directed, and halted immediately in rear of the right of the Nineteenth.

I presently met General Emory, who informed me that his lines were very much extended and very weak, and requested me to relieve the two brigades posted upon his right and enable him to strengthen his center. This I did at once, posting Colonel Well's brigade in the front line, with one regiment deployed as skirmishers in the woods along the margin of Red Bud Run. Colonel Harris' brigade formed the second line and had two regiments faced to the right and at right angles to the right of the line, these latter regiments in position occupied by a brigade of the Nineteenth Corps.

When these dispositions were made, General Sheridan arrived upon the ground and directed me, as soon as Colonel Duval's division arrived upon the opposite side of the morass, to move forward and charge the enemy and drive him from the woods in which he was posted, about 600 yards to my front. General Emory informed me that his corps had charged the enemy in this wood about an hour previous to my arrival and had been repulsed and driven back. A rousing cheer from the opposite side of Red Bud Run announced Colonel Duval's approach, and the order was at once given to move forward, which was done with alacrity. After moving about 300 yards through the open field, the enemy's artillery and musketry opened very briskly upon my lines, but its effect was to increase the impetuosity of the command, and with deafening yells and cheers the men rushed forward and reached the wood to find the enemy breaking and running in confusion.

A rapid pursuit was made, firing as briskly as possible and cheering most lustily. Deep ravines and entangling brushwood prevented the preservation of lines, and as the command emerged into the open country beyond, all technical order was gone, the two brigades were merged into a victorious throng, each individual of which was bent on pursuing and punishing the enemy, and all eagerly running and loading and firing and cheering. The enemy's left was entirely broken and we had passed beyond the left of his line that still remained intact, and were receiving from it a fire into our left flank and rear; the enemy had also turned toward the left, and from their retreating forces we also received a scattering fire. I directed a change of front to the left, but the instincts of the soldiers prompted the proper movement before my commands could be conveyed - each man was marching and facing toward the enemy's fire. Colonel Duval's command crossed the Red Bud Run or morass at this point, and his command and my own mingled together and acted together until the pursuit was over. Colonel Harris, commanding the Third Brigade, arrived with three regiments that had been formed on our right and now came forward very nearly unbroken. After facing to the left a succession of stone walls gave excellent cover to the enemy, and from behind them we received a very severe musketry fire, and at times suffered heavily from artillery, but we steadily advanced and beat back the enemy. The more advanced would take shelter behind a stone wall or such other protection as the irregularity of the surface of the land would afford; others would rush forward and take position beside these; soon a strong line would be formed and another advance made to the next stone wall or protection. After proceeding upward of a mile the Nineteenth Corps came up in our rear, and from that time forward assisted in driving the enemy.

My division claims the capture of one piece of artillery and two caissons, and with the Second Division was always in the advance until we entered Winchester in triumph. The conduct of officers and men was as a general thing deserving of the highest praise. I have never witnessed more zeal and daring than was here displayed. It is true our lines were broken and gone, but had we moved in such a manner as to preserve our lines the enemy would have escaped unhurt or else driven us back.

Individual acts of gallantry are too numerous to mention. I refer you to the reports of brigade and regimental commanders for details. I received invaluable assistance from Lieutenant Ballard, Macomber, Hornbrook, and Rollyson of my staff.[123] I lost four officers killed - Captain Thompson, Thirty-fourth Massachusetts Volunteers; Captain J.M. Ewing and Lieutenant C. B. McCollumn, of the Tenth West Virginia Volunteers, and Lieutenant Kirby, of the Eleventh West Virginia Volunteers, all good, brave officers. There were 17 officers wounded, 57 enlisted men were killed, 382 wounded, and 6 missing.[124]

I am, captain, very respectfully, your obedient servant,
J. THOBURN,
Colonel, Commanding
Captain P. G. BIER,
Assistant Adjutant-General, Dept. of West Virginia.

HEADQUARTERS FIRST INFANTRY DIVISION, ARMY OF WEST VIRGINIA, October 2, 1864.

CAPTAIN: I submit the following report of the part performed by the First Infantry Division at the battle of Fisher's Hill on the 22nd ultimo:

The Second Brigade of my division was still on duty at Winchester, the First and Third Brigades, commanded respectively by Cols. George D. Wells and T. H. Harris were, with the Second Division, held in reserve during the fore part of that day. About 2 o'clock in the afternoon, we were moved, under the supervision of General Crook, through woods and ravines, so as to be unobserved by the enemy, until we gained a position on the eastern slope of the Little North Mountain, upon the left of the enemy's line of works. The First Division moved by the right flank in two lines and to the left of the Second Division - Colonel Wells' brigade composing the first line and Colonel Harris' the second; our lines being at right angles to that of the enemy, which extended through the open field up the mountain slope to the edge of the woods, under the cover of which our troops were moving.

When the left of my line had nearly passed the left of the enemy's line of works the order was given "by the left flank," and the whole command moved in two lines down the slope to the edge of the woods. A few minutes before this the enemy had discovered our position and had commenced shelling us from their works on the opposite hill. The command emerged from the woods yelling and firing, and found the enemy running from their works in disorder. A vigorous pursuit was at once made, each man apparently vying with the others who could shout the loudest and fire the fastest. The open field for several hundred yards down the slope was interspersed with little clusters of field pines and briars, making serious obstacles to the advance of regular lines, and by the time the division had reached the foot of the hill, the lines were completely broken, and, as at the battle of Winchester, both brigades were merged into one large body of advancing soldiers, the bolder and stouter men being nearer the front, and the rear pushing forward and shouting and hurrahing and firing after the fast receding foe.

The pursuit was kept up without orders, and on the second hill we came to a pretty strong line of works that were extended rearward to the right to protect the enemy's left flank, which was carried without difficulty, and in which were captured three pieces of artillery. Fearing that we would come upon some strong fortified position of the enemy I, at this point, tried to arrest the advance of the division until the lines would be in a measure reformed and good order restored, but the bold, restive spirit of the men would not be repressed. While I would be stopping a few, others would break away, shouting and firing after the retreating enemy, so I had to abandon the idea of good order and lines and let them go ahead. On approaching the next hill, which was covered with woods, the enemy endeavored to make a more stubborn resistance, and our advance for a short time was driven back, but the rear soon closed up and General Crook, approaching at the time and cheering the men forward, a rush was made up the steep acclivity and the enemy again routed and more guns captured.

At this point, we were joined by the Third Division of the Sixth Corps, and throughout the remainder of the charge the men and officers of both commands mingled together in one body. The Second Division of the Army of West Virginia had previously to this mingled with the First Division. The charge was continued until the pike was reached and we advanced along the pike one mile to Round Top Mountain, when a halt was made, the enemy being then out of hearing. The command was fairly exhausted, having made a charge of five miles in length. After a half hour's cheering and congratulating the men laid down and slept without dinner, supper, or blankets, having stripped themselves before the engagement.

The advance was made in rear of the enemy's works. The prisoners and guns that were captured were left for others to pick up. Two battle-flags were captured by men of my division. My loss was 1 officer killed, 1 enlisted man killed, and 77 wounded. Officers and men, with few exceptions, behaved with great gallantry, and are deserving of highest praise.[125]

>I have the honor to be, very respectfully, your most obedient servant,
>   J. THOBURN,
>   Colonel, Commanding.
>   Captain P. G. BIER,
>   Assistant Adjutant-General.

On October 3, 1864, sketch artist James E. Taylor, attached to Sheridan's army for Frank Leslie's Illustrated Newspaper, visited Maj. Gen. George Crook's headquarters about one mile south of the courthouse in Harrisonburg and sketched the above scene which included Thoburn, second from left speaking to the mounted Major John R. Meigs of Sheridan's staff. Meigs would be killed by Confederates near Dayton later that day. Also, in the picture from the far right are: George Crook, seated; Adj. Philip Bier, formerly of the 1st West Virginia; Col. William C. Starr, seated; and standing to his immediate left, looking toward Meigs, Capt. William McKinley, later the 25th president of the United States. Dick Shelley, a war correspondent for the Baltimore American, stands grasping the flagpole. The officer between McKinley and Shelly is unidentified as are the other mounted officers toward the back. James E. Taylor Sketchbook: With Sheridan up the Shenandoah Valley in 1864: Leaves from a Special Artist's Sketchbook and Diary. The Western Reserve Historical Society, Cleveland, Ohio.

From firsthand experience, Thoburn had seen Union forces achieve success in the Valley only to have it quickly reversed. Under Sheridan, however, the triumph was permanent. After Fisher's Hill, the U.S. Army of the Shenandoah pursued Jubal Early's Confederate Army of the Valley District to the environs of Harrisonburg where the main part of the Union army encamped. Early's troops retreated to Brown's Gap in the Blue Ridge where he was reinforced by Maj. Gen. Joseph B. Kershaw's infantry division, Maj. Wilfred E. Cutshaw's Artillery Battalion and Brig. Gen. Thomas Rosser's cavalry brigade. Although greatly needed, these additions did not make up the more than 5,200 men Early had lost since the battles of Third Winchester and Fisher's Hill.

While Sheridan's infantry remained at Harrisonburg, his cavalry pursued to Early and engaged elements of his army at Port Republic, Waynesboro and other locales. Sheridan did not go after the Confederates or attempt to cross the Blue Ridge and threaten Richmond from the west. On September 29, Sheridan telegraphed Grant, "I think the best policy will be to let the burning of the crops of the Valley be the end of this campaign, and let some of this army go somewhere else." As Sheridan's army slowly withdrew down the Valley toward Winchester, the Union cavalry spread out across the valley and systematically burned the crops in the fields, barns and mills and drove off all the livestock before them, leaving the Valley "a barren waste" as Grant had directed.[126]

While none of Thoburn's extant writings detail the fall campaign in the Valley in the thorough manner as did his spring and summer journal, the following letter to his brother Thomas provides some bigger picture perspectives. Thomas, an officer in the 50th Ohio, had just completed his participation in Maj. Gen. William T. Sherman's capture of Atlanta. Of particulate note, is Jospeh Thoburn's acceptance of the "burning" as a tactic in the Valley. Previously, Thoburn had taken a dim view of Maj. Gen. David Hunter's retaliatory burnings of individual homes. In the fall of 1864, Thoburn recognized its value as a war measure and seemed to share Sheridan's philosophy. "If I had a barn full of wheat and a son, I would much sooner lose the barn and the wheat than my son." This letter also reveals Thoburn's motivation for serving his country and the deep pride he took in commanding a division in Crook's Army of West Virginia.[127]

Harrisonburg, Va
Oct. 4, 1864

My Dear Brother,

Yours of Sept. 19th is rec'd. I have papers with me pertaining to the organization of the 1st Va. Inf. and am therefore unable to give Capt. Morgan the data asked for. I once furnished him with invoices of what he rec'd, and he can get his receipts for the same at the Ordnance Dep't at Washington, D.C. Tell him I would be pleased to give him the information asked for, but it wasn't in my power.

We are quietly resting here. The enemy has been reinforced by two Divisions of Infantry and is lying between us and Staunton. I do not believe he is strong enough to attack us, and Sheridan does not on his part show disposition to attack. I think his policy will be to try and induce the rebels to follow him down the valley where he can fight them to a better advantage and where in case of disaster escape will be more difficult to them. From all we hear the rebel army is very much demoralized, desertions are very frequent, and despondency great.

Genl. Sheridan is destroying all the grain, hay, and stock of this valley, leaving nothing whatever. He is determined that no rebel army shall subsist in this valley nor draw any subsistence from it. The citizens are in great distress. Many families are moving north in our returning empty trains. Others whose sympathies are in the other direction will have to go south, for starvation and famine will surely rest upon this garden spot of the state. There are a great many good union families in this neighborhood. To destroy as we are doing is a very painful duty, but it is believed to be a military necessity and "the end will justify the means" which though not a very good rule for an individual man, may do in war, for all elements of war are evils. The taking of life is certainly worse than the destruction of property.

Our army is in excellent spirits and full of hope and confidence. McClellanism[128] is nowhere here; none but bummers and skulkers talk of him. Our late victories have not been exaggerated in the papers. The victory was in each case complete – but I notice that Genl. Crook's command has not rec'd the credit that is due. It was our command that in both battles broke the enemies [sic] lines and commenced the route. Others only came in after us through the breach we had made. This is a simple fact, let reports be what they may. No one gainsays it here. I am sorry to hear from David [Thoburn's brother]. His dropsical affliction is a complication I don't well understand. I trust he may be gratified with being elected [Auditor of Belmont County, Ohio]. I expect to be home about the 13th of next month.

Genl. Crook and Sheridan have, I understand, both petitioned for my promotion, but I do not expect anything from it. And if I should be promoted, it will only be a Brevetship which would not retain me beyond my three years of service. The War Dep't has assigned three different Brig. Genls. to my command, but Genl Crook has given three little commands about Harpers Ferry and on the [B & O] railroad, and still retains me in command of a division while quite a number of Brigadiers are here commanding brigades.[129] This is as much a of a compliment to myself as I could ask, and certainly a much greater complement than the commission that these others bear. I would rather not retire from the service, and had hoped that Gov. Boreman [of West Virginia] would have filled my Reg't so that I might have retained. But my principle has been to do what was asked of me and seek nothing more. And when my country asks nothing more of me, I should not hesitate to retire.[130]

Give my love to Janette and Jane.

> Very truly yours,
> J. Thoburn

On October 9, Sheridan's assumption about the combat ability of Early's army was strengthened when the Union cavalry routed Rosser with Early's entire cavalry force at the battle of Tom's Brook, capturing hundreds of prisoners and eleven pieces of artillery. At this point, Sheridan's Army of the Shenandoah encamped along the banks of Cedar Creek and the campaign was seemingly at its end. However, Early was not done. On October 13 he conducted a reconnaissance in force that resulted in the death of Col. George D. Wells, commanding the First Brigade of Thoburn's division. Six days later, Early's infantry conducted an arduous night march, much of it along the side of Massanutten Mountain, and launched a pre-dawn surprise attack against Sheridan that routed two-thirds of his army. Sheridan had been at Washington for a couple of days and had spent the previous night at Winchester. Hearing the sounds of battle, he rapidly rode to the battlefield, rallied his troops and launched a counterattack that swept the Confederates from the field and permanently ended Confederate power in the Valley.

On the night of October 18-19, 1864, Col. Thoburn slept in an ambulance at his hilltop headquarters behind the entrenched lines of his division. In the early morning darkness, Capt. Hamilton L. Karr, a self-described early riser, heard picket firing and woke Lt. Col. Thomas F. Wildes of the 116th Ohio and warned him of the apparent threat. Wildes promptly roused the troops of his brigade and ordered them into the breastworks. The firing from the picket line intensified, and Karr galloped back to Thoburn's headquarters and found him asleep in the ambulance. Karr roused Thoburn from his slumber and informed him of the developing situation. The drowsy West Virginian muttered back, "That cannot be." As Karr assured Thoburn that it was, the rattle of a dozen more musket shots rang out, prompting the staff officer to ask, "Did you hear that?" The gunfire jarred Thoburn to full awareness of the situation, and he quickly readied himself for action, mounted his horse and galloped toward the front. He quickly discovered that his command had been overrun, rallied some men at the western end of their camp and fought a brief but futile delaying action before being overwhelmed and forced into a chaotic retreat. Thoburn raced his horse toward the Valley Pike where he worked in vain to rally his men.[131]

By 6:00 a.m., the tide of defeated troops had carried Thoburn into Middletown. There he struggled to disentangle the confused wagons and rally fleeing soldiers in the streets of Middletown. Confederate cavalry dashed among the wagon trains in a most chaotic scene. In the early morning darkness and fog, a rebel wearing a blue Federal uniform ordered Thoburn to halt. He thought the soldier a Union cavalryman, paid him no heed, and continued his fruitless attempts to bring order out of the confusion. In fact, Thoburn did not realize that the demand for surrender was directed at him, but the Virginian nevertheless fired a point blank shot from his revolver. The bullet struck his left side, piercing both lungs and knocking Thoburn from his horse, slamming

The Foul Murder of Colonel Thoburn in the Streets of Middletown.
James E. Taylor Sketchbook: With Sheridan up the Shenandoah Valley in 1864: Leaves from a Special Artist's Sketchbook and Diary.
The Western Reserve Historical Society, Cleveland, Ohio.

him into the ground where he laid in agony for ten minutes. Mrs. Mary E. Hoover of Middletown saw him gasping on the ground and ventured out of her house to render what aid she could. Lying upon the ground in an awkward manner that heightened the pain, Thoburn asked that she turn him over, which she did with the assistance of a kind Confederate soldier who stopped to assist. He asked that Mary tell Kate that his only "regret was to leave his wife and children. O, he said, how I would love to see them here. He said he was prepared for death, prepared to meet his God. He told me to give you a dying farewell, and for you all to meet him in heaven where there would be no more parting." Before long, artillery shells began to rain on the village and Mrs. Hoover took shelter in her cellar, leaving the colonel outside. When the action in the village cooled off, a gentleman of Middletown assisted her in carrying him into his house. After the U. S. forces regained the town, Thoburn's comrades found him, and a surgeon pronounced the wound mortal, saying he would not live through the night. The stoic colonel replied that "the news did not shock him in the least that he had known after the first ten minutes his wound was mortal, and he was ready to meet his fate." He passed from this world at 12:02 a.m. on October 20, 1864.[132]

His death saddened the soldiers who had served under his command. Private Charles Lynch of the 18th Connecticut had served under Thoburn from New Market to Berryville. When he learned of his death, he wrote, "We are all sorry that he was killed. He was one of the best officers in our corps. Colonel Thoburn, 1st West Virginia Regiment, a good friend to our regiment, a medical doctor by profession."[133]

When Thoburn's remains arrived in Wheeling, he was dressed in a citizen's clothes and transferred to the home of James Wilson, a former officer in the 1st West Virginia and the husband of Thoburn's oldest sister Jeanette, for a viewing. There the family received friends and family who gazed upon his face one last time. One visitor, nineteen year-old Sergeant Stockton Carmack, had served under Thoburn since 1861. In 1864, he had been the Colonel's orderly until he had been wounded at the Battle of Snickers Gap on July 18, 1864. Carmack had earned a solid reputation for bravery on the battlefield, but when he saw his fallen commander, he "burst into convulsive sobs and moans, giving evidence of deep distress," that greatly affected everyone who was present.[134]

At the time of Thoburn's death, Maj. Gen. Samuel Heintzleman, former commander of the Army of the Potomac's Third Army Corps, was stationed in Wheeling. Heintzleman extensively detailed Thoburn's funeral proceedings in his journal:

> October 25, 1864: This has been quite a pleasant day. At 2 P.M., the procession was formed for the funeral of Col. Thoburn, Captain Philip G. Bier [Assistant Adjutant General for General George Crook] and Sergeant Jenkins – the two former killed at Cedar Creek. Gen. Benjamin F. Kelley, myself, Col. William G. Ely, Major Daniel H. McPhail were the pallbearers for Col. Thoburn.[135] The bodies lay in the Senate chamber under a canopy of flags and were taken to the Methodist Church where the services were held. The Rev. Mr. Moffat, a Presbyterian, made one of the finest, loyal addresses I ever heard. The Rev. Dr. Drummond is not well, but he followed with an excellent short address.

The cemetery, "Mt. Wood," is on one of the highest points on the heights above the city. The whole population of the city and much from the surrounding country attended. There were thousands in and around the cemetery. I seldom witnessed a more impressive ceremony. I was pleased to see the Presbyterians and Methodists fraternizing… There were many Copperheads to hear the loyal addresses.[136]

For Mrs. Thoburn the grief of losing her husband and raising their children alone remained a lifelong burden. On December 13, 1864, the anniversary of the Thoburns's wedding, she added this somewhat prophetic entry in the back of his journal:

Eleven years ago this day, I was married to the writer of this book. A nobler and braver man never lived. On the 19th of October, he sacrificed his life to his country. With three little children of our love, I am left to mourn my great and irreparable loss. My heart is torn, and I feel that all is gone. He was my idol, my strong support. On him I rested. O' what shall I do now? How great my responsibility. Where will I be when eleven more years pass 'round? Perhaps I with my beloved. May God grant that when death comes to me I may join him and may our family be unbroken.[137]

Kate soon moved back to Mount Pleasant in Belmont County, on the Ohio side of the Ohio River where she moved in with her family. There, she raised the children, ages four, six, and eight (at the time of his death) with the help of her family and a Widow's Pension from Joseph's army service. She lived there until her death in 1888 when her earthly remains joined her husband in eternal rest at Mt. Wood Cemetery overlooking Wheeling.

This house sits on the location described by special sketch artist James E. Taylor as the home where Thoburn died. Frederick County tax records indicate that this house was built in 1859 so, if Taylor's description is accurate, this is likely the house where Thoburn died. However, the house that Taylor sketched was constructed of logs and appears smaller. It would not be uncommon for the home to have been expanded and for siding to be added over the original logs during the process.

PROLOGUE 113

Western Union Telegraph from Benjamin Rush Cowen, who was the adjutant general of Ohio at the time, and married to Thoburn's sister, Ellen. The telegraph was to Thoburn's sister, Eliza, informing her of his death. Suzanne Pezick Collection.

*Captain Philip G. Bier, 12th West Virginia Infantry,
served as assistant adjutant general on General Crook's staff.
He was also killed on October 19, 1864, at the Battle of Cedar Creek.
Photo courtesy of Richard A. Wolfe.*

Daily Intelligencer.

CAMPBELL & M'DERMOT,
PROPRIETORS AND EDITORS.

TERMS.—DAILY, delivered in city per week, 15 cents
DAILY, by mail, in advance,................$8.00
TRI-WEEKLY, in advance,..................5.00
WEEKLY, in advance,......................2.00
WEEKLY, six months,......................1.00

Wednesday Morning, October 26.

Funeral Obsequies of Col. Thoburn, Capt. Bier and Sergeant Jenkins, —The City in Mourning.

In accordance with previous arrangements the funeral obsequies of Col. Joseph Thoburn, Capt. Phillip Bier and Sergeant Benjamin Jenkins, of the 1st West Virginia Cavalry, took place yesterday afternoon.— The city was draped in mourning. Flags at half mast, bearing emblems of mourning were hanging from the residences and places of business of our loyal people, who thus saw proper to testify their sorrow for the loss of the dead heroes who had fought their last battle and were about to be conveyed to their last resting place.

The Daily Intelligencer in Wheeling, West Virginia, describes the city in mourning for Thoburn, Bier, and Sgt. Benjamin Jenkins of the 1st West Virginia Cavalry. Jenkins died of wounds received on September 5, 1864, at Bunker Hill, West Virginia.

*Grave of Colonel Joseph Thoburn.
Mount Wood Cemetery, Wheeling, West Virginia.
Photo courtesy of Richard A. Wolfe.*

Appendix A

Letters from the 1st West Virginia Infantry and Colonel Joseph Thoburn

These letters are intended to give the reader the perspective of soldiers in Thoburn's command in several key actions in the Shenandoah Valley Campaign, including two from the campaign against Confederate Maj. Gen. Thomas J. "Stonewall" Jackson in 1862.

∽ ∾

Battle of Kernstown
Wheeling Daily Intelligencer, April 2, 1862

"From Our 1st Virginia Regiment,"

The battle near Winchester, on the 23d instant was for the time of its continuance one of the most fiercely contested actions of the war. The rebel forces under [Thomas J.] Jackson were evidently misled by their friends in the neighborhood as to the number of the Union forces. They were confident of victory. They were, without doubt, to supper that night in Winchester, with their secesh friends, from whom they had lately departed in evacuating the place. From the statements of rebel prisoners, and from the other evidences, whiskey was freely distributed to their forces upon the commencement of the attack. It needed but one bold dash, and their old position with all the honors of the achievement, was to be theirs. How signally this whole program failed, the telegraph has already informed you.

The position of the enemy in the afternoon was admirably chosen. Gen. Erastus Tyler's third brigade found a large [Confederate] force posted behind of the stone fences with which this country abounds by the and which are almost impregnable to any attack except that of artillery. Other forces were placed in the rear of this, and ascending the slope at intervals to the top, where their artillery was placed. Tyler's brigade advanced upon the enemy [in column] in the following order: 7th Ohio, 7th Indiana, 1st Virginia, 110th Pennsylvania, and 29th Ohio. Companies A and G of the 1st Virginia were deployed to the left as skirmishers.[138] The Union forces reached to within about 100 yards of the rebels strongly entrenched behind the stone fence, before either side seemed to be aware of the other's presence. And it was here, directly facing each other, and almost in sight of the whites of each other's eyes, that the deadly conflict raged for over two hours. It was pending this struggle that Col. Thoburn, of the 1st Virginia, placing his cap on the point of his sword, and waving it to his men, called upon them to follow him in a dash across the open field, and directly fronting the enemy's fire, for the purpose of gaining a position on his flank. It was a severe ordeal; but nobly did the 1st Virginia boys endure it. Of the five men killed in this regiment, four fell during this deployment. Others, of whom Col. Thoburn himself was one, were wounded at the same time. But it is perhaps scarcely too much to say that the movement saved the brigade, and turned the fortunes of the day. The rebels soon gave way in the face of the flank fire and the direct fire in front. As the rebels commenced to retreat, the 14th Indiana was brought up on our left, and aided materially in completing the rout. Night soon after closed in, putting an end for the time to the conflict.

Major Isaac H. Duval's horse was shot under him, pierced by half a dozen balls during the first round.[139] The cool courage and soldierly bearing of this officer during the entire engagement was the theme of universal commendation. The other field and company officers of the regiment behaved valiantly throughout the fight, and the entire regiment, in this the first battle in which many of them were ever engaged, displayed an intrepid valor not often surpassed by veterans. Their friends at home have reason to be proud of them. These remarks are not to be taken as disparaging others of the Union forces when all acted bravely. The slaughter was terrific. Rebel prisoners who were in the fight at Bull Run say that there was no such desperate courage displayed there as here.

G. B.

~ ~

Battle of Port Republic
Wheeling Daily Intelligencer, June 20, 1862
Letter from the First Virginia Regiment
Luray, Page County, Va.
June 11, 1862

Dear Father:

We have had another battle accompanied with a retreat, and again the 1st Virginia has met face-to-face the rebel hordes who dare assail our flag. This time, Wellsburg mourns the loss of several of her brave lads.

I wrote to you on Friday last from Honeyville. On the same evening Gen. Shields came up to our camp and had a long consultation with Colonel Thoburn who as then in command of the regiments stationed there, belonging to the 4th brigade. On Saturday morning, we moved up the river to join Col. Carroll, with the 7th Indiana, then at Naked Creek. We joined them in the afternoon and all moved up several miles further, four miles above Conrad's Store.[140] This was ten miles from Port Republic and eighteen from our camp of the the day before. At 1 o'clock Sunday morning we started on a miserable road, through a long, low dark woods, a literal "slough of despond" and the "valley of the shadow of death" to many a poor fellow. At about 10 o'clock we came in sight of Port Republic, a small village on the north side of the Shenandoah. On the hills back of the village could be seen Jackson's baggage train and camps with his artillery. Soon our cannon commenced shelling one of their camps, they replying from two pieces away off to the right.

Our object was to cross the river here and destroy their baggage, fall back across the river and proceed up to Waynesborough and burn two railroad bridges, thus completely cutting off Jackson's communication and retreat. Well, the cavalry under Col. Carroll and Major

Chamberlain made a dash into the bridge, the infantry, four small regiments, following close up. By this time we had gone for half a mile along Jackson's line, and the rebels could be seen plainly maneuvering on the opposite side of the river, when almost simultaneously, the rebels unmasked and opened on us nineteen more pieces of cannon. Of course this made things so hot that we could not stand it, and we "about faced" and fell back a couple of miles. In this cannonading our regiment did not lose a man, but the brigade lost about twenty. Captain Robinson lost three pieces of artillery, which got swamped. The 3rd Brigade came up in the evening, and we bivouacked in sight of the enemy.

The next morning was foggy, but so soon as it became clear enough for sight, the enemy could be seen advancing on our position up the road and alone the bottom. We fell in and formed on the road, and two of our cannon on the left, placed on the edge of a road, commenced shelling the approaches to our position. We moved up into the woods to support this battery, which kept firing away with great effect. The rebels replied to this fire bringing into action quite a number of guns. Directly the forces down in the bottom on our right engaged, infantry and artillery. From our place we could see distinctly how the fight was going on. Our men drove the secesh back with heavy loss, and with sufficient force, could have whipped them to death, but the rebels were too may for us as their replacements could be seen plainly coming up in large numbers. To counteract this, our regiments were ordered down into the open fields.

We soon engaged the enemy at fair rifle range. They could not stand this increased fire and divining the defenceless state of our left, fell back from the bottom into the woods, our men closely chasing them the 1st Virginia in the lead. In less than five minutes they made their appearance on our left, in strong force, under cover of the woods, pouring a heavy fire into our men, and charged and took our left battery of two pieces. To check this flank movement, which had it been successful, would have cut us all off, the 7th Indiana and 7th Ohio marched up to meet this storm of hail, and right gallantly they stood up to the work. The battery was retaken, but the rebels reinforced again, and we all formed under a heavy fire to fall back. This we did, starting in good order, but the enemy threw the shell into us so heavy that no line could be kept in order. The cavalry made four or five charges on our rear, killing and capturing several. The order of retreat was for the 29th Ohio to cover the rear. This regiment was nearly all captured and killed, or the rest scattered. This threw the 1st Virginia into the rear. I saw every charge they made. They had one piece of artillery with them and we had several, but they had not a single round of ammunition. We fell back rapidly twelve miles, when we met reinforcements, and the secesh halted, Fremont having attacked them in rear.

The forces engaged on our side were the 3rd and 4th Brigades, the first consisting of the 5th, 7th, 29th and 66th Ohio, about 2,000 strong; the second of the 1st Virginia, 7th Indiana, 84th and 110th Pennsylvania, about 800 strong. We were pitted against Jackson's whole army about 35,000 strong, and how we made the stand we did, is more than I can tell. Our regiment went into Sunday's fight 205 strong, and when we counted off in the evening we numbered 118! Since then we have picked up a good many, and I am enabled to give you a fair estimate of the loss of Companies G and B. I will give you the loss of the regiment in another letter. Co. B has George Prather, wounded and prisoner, George Taylor, LaGrange, James Caball (from up Buffalo), Thos. Merryman and Joseph Noland missing. Co. G. Has Sam'l. Callendilne, Jno. Adams, Wellsburg, and John Edie and Daniel Kerr, Hancock County missing.[141]

I was in the fight all through both day's work. The only mark I have is a scratch from a piece of shell thrown into my face, which burst just at my left. The dirt and dust blinded me so that I could not see for some time. A piece of the shell struck a sergeant just in front of me, shivering his gun to pieces and making an ugly place in his side. He was so close that I could have put my hand on him. Major Duval is wounded in the leg and starts for home tomorrow. I marched twenty miles of the retreat in my bare feet, my shoes having given out, but I must close.

Write soon. Direct to Lurary.
Lt. Henry J. Johnson

The following letter is taken from Major Thomas C. Thoburn's *My Experiences During the Civil War.* This work was published by Lyle Thoburn in Cleveland, Ohio, in 1963. This letter from his brother, Colonel Joseph Thoburn, describes northern Virginia during the war and shares his thoughts on the conduct of the war and recent events:

Clouds Mill near Alexandria
July 7, 1862

My Dear Brother Thomas,

Having an hour of leisure, I give it to you. At this season of the year you have much less leisure than I. Harvest and cherries are upon you. But you have a long hour of rest in the cool shade at noon and will be able to read my short epistle. I have written a good many letters to Kate addressing them to her at St. Clairsville, but from the last I recd from her she had not left Mt. P[leasant] as soon as she expected. Perhaps by this time she is there. Wheat harvest is over here some time ago, but there is but little wheat in this country to cut.

It is a most beautiful country from here out towards Manassas and up the river beyond Washington as far as I have seen. But desolation is all around us, fencing destroyed, barns dilapidated, houses ditto. The blight of the Army is everywhere seen. Very few of the old citizens remain here. None whatever of the leading or influential class, except you include widows & very aged people. This is true of most of the country that we have passed over. One thing you never see [is] men at home capable of bearing arms.

All that are fit to make soldiers have been drafted into the Southern Army or have followed their army voluntarily. I have not seen enough of young men since leaving Winchester to form a single company. The Southern Army is now full. They will never be able to have another such. There force is much larger than ours. We have considerably less than 300,000 men in the field. I do not think that McClelland [sic] had over 70,000 men and at the least calculation the Rebels had 150,000 against him. The best thing our government has done is the call for 300,000 more men. With that many more men we can finish up the work even should England and France interfere.

I am beginning to despair of restoring the Union. The Southern heart is so embittered against us that it will require years to bring about amicable relations which are essential to a true union. But While I despair of a restoration of the Union, I do not despair of a complete & triumphant victory to our Arms. We must whip them & whip them badly, and we will do it. Southern arrogance would be unbearable unless we did it. Had we good generalship it wound have been done long ago. But I expect better generalship from this to the close of the war than we have had, & if I am not badly mistaken most of the hard fighting is yet to take place.

Our Brigade is in camp here with the reserve Army Corps – and may possibly be here a month yet until we will up our numbers. But everything connected with our future is very uncertain. The commander of this Brigade remains in Washington & being the next in rank according to Seniority, I have to command in his absence. Were it not for this, I would have been in Wheeling on recruiting service to fill up the reg't. The order came to go, but I could not get relieved from the command of the Brigade. It may be that I will be sent down for a few days to superintend the operations of those now there.

If I get down, I expect to see you all. But while affairs remain as they are here, I would be ashamed to be seen at home. The amount of shoulder straps that are hanging around good hotels & loitering away from the service is a disgrace to us, and I have no idea of adding to it. Our Army is not that pure self-sacrificing body that our orators and correspondents would have us believe. Many of the officers are place seekers and politicians, & the great majority of the soldiers comes from the very lowest walks of society. This being the case, it is impossible to have success and honor always attend us. But all armies are alike in this respect and we are good as any other army in the World, and perhaps a great deal better.

We have pure and noble leaders among us. I feel like placing Genl. McClelland at the head of the list. The time was when I with a great many others felt like distrusting him, but his later conduct has amply vindicated him. He is not brilliant as Napoleon, but he is safe and reliable. His proclamation of the 4th is a masterpiece. In the late 8 days fighting he was whipped and driven back. This is the plain English of it – yet during the battles his army conducted themselves so gallantly that they gave harder blows than they rec'd and are today in better spirits than those who drove them.

If you have an hour of leisure let me hear from you and tell Mother that a letter from her would be most acceptable. It is a long time since I rec'd one from her. I know it is very difficult for her to write. Since I left I have frequently thought she should consult Dr. Alex or Dr. Bates, or some other one about her stomach. I do wish she would do it. If Eliza is home tell her that I have rec'd no answer to my last letter, and I would like so much to see a line from Mary and Bella. Love to you all.

Affectionately Your Brother,
Joseph Thoburn[142]

Appendix B

Colonel Thoburn's Report on the Battle of Piedmont

Headquarters 2nd Brigade
1st Infantry Div. Dept. W. Va.[143]

Captain:

I have the honor of submitting to you the following report of the part taken by the 2nd brigade in the battle at Piedmont June 5th, 1864.
This brigade approached the battle field marching by the flank, three hundred paces to the left of the road and in the following order: 1st W. Va. Infantry, Lt. Col. Jacob Weddle; 2nd Eastern Shore Md. Infantry, Col. R. S. Rodgers; 34th Mass Vol. Infantry, Col. Geo. D. Wells; 12th W. Va. Infantry, Col. Wm. B. Curtis and 54th Pa Vol. Infantry. The 4th W. Va. Infantry, Col. J. H. Dayton was detailed as rear guard to the wagon train. At 8:30 o'clock A. M. when the head of the column was coming within range of the enemy's guns, I was directed to form the Brigade in two lines and move forward. When the advance regiment (1st W. Va. Infantry) was formed in line I was directed to move it forward in line with the first line of the 1st Brigade, which was then resting immediately on its right (This regiment by following the movements of the 1st Brigade was separated from my command and did not join us until after the battle). The 12th W. Va. and the 34th Mass composed my first line and 2nd Md and 54th Pa the second line. I

moved forward on the left of the road under cover of a belt of woodland, one mile in advance of the 1st Brigade to an open field in our front, upon the opposite side of which the Enemy had erected barricades of fence rails extending three-fourths of a mile in length behind which the enemy was seen. I sent back an Aide to report the situation and ask for orders.

In the meantime, the enemy had discovered our situation and were shelling us from the open ground in our front and right but without inflicting much injury. My Aide returned with orders to hold my ground until the 1st Brigade advanced. On watching the 1st Brigade, I observed it moving forward in line to attack the enemy who was in cover of a woods to its front and saw it repulsed and falling back; and a shout along the rebel line to our front indicated that the day was going against us.

Knowing that I was doing no good where I was and that I should be needed on the right, I at once gave orders to fall back by alternate battalions which was done until we arrived opposite the 1st Brigade where I took position supporting Dupont's and Carlin's Batteries and awaited orders. I had been there but a few minutes when I received orders from General Hunter to leave one regiment in support of the Batteries and move across the Valley to the right and attack the enemy in the woods on their right flank. The 2nd Md. Was left in position and the 54th Pa., 34th Mass., and the 12th W. Va. moved forward and formed lines of battle, charged into the woods and drove the enemy from his position capturing several hundred prisoners and two stand of colors. Among the killed who fell in this charge was Brig. Genl. W. E. Jones who commanded the enemy's forces. When I was charging on the enemy's right, the 1st W. Va on the right of the 1st Brigade charged forward and cooperating with the three regiments on the left in driving the enemy from the field and captured the colors of the 31st Va. Rebel Infantry, making three stand of colors captured by my brigade.[144]

The officers and men of my Brigade without exception behaved well and all are deserving of high commendation but I would call especial attention to the gallant conduct of Col. J. M. Campbell of the 54th Pa, Col. W. B. Curtis 12th W. Va. and Col. Geo. D. Wells of the 34th Mass., who by their courage and energy contributed largely to the triumph of the final charge. While all the members of my staff did well, I would mention the name of my Acting Assistant Adjutant Genl. Lt. J. H. Rider who assisted me in the most important manner, exhibiting a cool daring and quick intelligence that is worthy of all praise. The total loss in the Brigade was thirty-six (36) enlisted men killed, Seven (7) officers and two-hundred and two (202) enlisted men wounded, and two (2) missing. I refer you to the reports of the regimental commanders for details.

                        I am Captain
                        Very Respectfullly
                        Your Obedient Servant,
                        J. Thoburn
                        Colonel.

Appendix C

Accounts of Thoburn's Death

The following letters provide eyewitness accounts of Thoburn's last hours on earth, including a poignant letter from Mrs. Mary Hoover of Middletown to Kate Thoburn and another from a staff officer.

❧ ❧

Middletown, Frederick County

Dear Friend,

It is with a heavy heart that I sit down to drop a few lines. It was the request of your dying husband. I was by his side about ten minutes after he fell. I did all I could for him. He asked me to turn him over which I did with the assistance of a Confederate soldier, who was very kind to him. When he was turned over, he told me to take hold of his hand. He asked me to write to you. I told him I would, he told me that all his regret was to leave his wife and children. O, he said how I would love to see them here. He said he was prepared for death, prepared to meet his God. He told me to give you a dying farewell, and for you all to meet him in heaven where there would be no more parting. Your husband did not die for want of care. He has paid the debt we all have to pay and is now a bright Angel around the Throne of our heavenly father,

> Your friend,
> Mrs. Mary E. Hoover[145]

❧ ☙

"How Col. Thoburn Was Killed"
By Captain Reed

He was shot just under the lower rib, in the left side, and the ball passed out a little higher up on the right side, apparently with the junction of the ribs with the spinal column. Capt Reed informed us that both lungs had been penetrated and that the loss of blood had been very great. The circumstances of Col. Thoburn's death, as related by Capt. Thomas Reed [Thoburn's aide-de-camp] are as follows:

> He was killed about six o'clock on Wednesday morning. The enemy had burst in upon his division, which occupied the extreme front, about 3 o'clock that morning and as the dispatches have already shown, had surprised and overpowered it. It had been driven steadily back as far as Middletown, indeed through that place. Col. Thoburn, at the time of his death was busily engaged disentangling and pushing forward his retreating [wagon] trains. The rebel cavalry had flanked the left of our army, and in large numbers had come in on our trains, attacking them fiercely. One of them dressed in our uniform rode up to Col. Thoburn and commanded him to halt. The Colonel not knowing the rebel was a foe, in fact not knowing that it was himself being addressed, did not halt, and accordingly, the cavalryman fired, the ball taking effect as we have stated.
>
> He fell from his horse at the side of the street on a vacant lot where he there remained for a miserable time according to the statement of a lady who had paid him some attention while lying there. She was compelled to leave him by reason of the danger to her person from the exploding shells, and c., and took herself to her cellar. A gentleman of the place, after the battle had lulled a

little, took the Colonel into his house and had him cared for in a passable way. It was in this house that Captain Reed found him about dusk in the evening. He was sensible all the time up to two minutes past twelve that night at which time he died.

He suffered excessively toward the last half hour, yet managed to talk at times, and was perfectly resigned and calm. As soon as Captain Reed found him, he sent off and called in the Medical Director, who hastily examined the wound and pronounced it mortal, and stated his hope that the Colonel would survive it. Colonel Thoburn, himself a physician, merely shook his head, saying nothing. The surgeon of the 10th West Virginia Infantry was called in, and he without hesitation decided that the wound was mortal and that the sufferer could not live overnight. When this was told Colonel Thoburn, he replied that the news did not shock him in the least, that he had known after the first ten minutes his wound was mortal and that he was ready to meet his fate.

In reply to a question whether he had any messages to send home, he requested Captain Reed to take down some directions about his worldly affairs, and then after they had been penned and read over to him, Thoburn said, "Tell my wife not to grieve for me, and my children to be good and true." These are the last words he spoke.[146]

Bibliography

Joseph Thoburn Collection, Suzanne Pezick.

Hennessy, John. *Second Manassas Battlefield Study*. Lynchburg: H.E. Howard, 2nd Edition.

Knight, Charles R. *Valley Thunder: The Battle of New Market and the Opening of the Shenandoah Valley Campaign, May 1864*. New York and CA: Savas Beattie LLC, 2010.

Lynch, Charles, *The Civil War Diary of Charles H. Lynch, 18th Connecticut Infantry Volunteers*. Hartford: Case, Lockwood & Brainard Co., 1915.

Newton, J. H., Nichols, G. G., and Sprankle, A. G. *History of the Panhandle; Being Collections of the Counties of Ohio, Brooke, Marshall and Hancock, West Virginia*. Wheeling: L. A. Caldwell, 1879.

Patchan, Scott C. *The Battle of Piedmont and Hunter's Raid on Staunton, The 1864 Valley Campaign*. Charleston: The History Press, 2011.

Patchan, Scott C. *The Forgotten Fury: The Battle of Piedmont, Va*. Fredericksburg: Sgt. Kirkland's Press, 1996.

Patchan, Scott C. *The Last Battle of Winchester: Philip Sheridan, Jubal Early and the Shenandoah Valley Campaign August 7-September 19, 1864.* New York and CA: Savas Beattie LLC, 2013.

Patchan, Scott C. *Shenandoah Summer: The 1864 Valley Campaign.* Lincoln and London: University of Nebraska Press, 2007.

Rawling, Charles J. *History of the First Regiment West Virginia Infantry.*

Thoburn, C. Stanley. *The Ancestry of the Irish-American Thoburns.* Cleveland: Thomas W. Thoburn and Benjamin W. Fauver, 1955.

U.S. War Department, The Official Records of the War of the Rebellion. Volumes 37 and 43.

Newspapers

Wheeling Daily Intelligencer

Wheeling Weekly Register

Notes

Introduction

1. The 1st West Virginia Infantry was raised in 1861 like other regiments that were recruited in the area that later became the state of West Virginia. Officially, it was known as the 1st Virginia Volunteer Infantry serving in the United States Army. When West Virginia became a separate state in 1863, the regiment, like all units from the Mountain State, officially became known as a "West Virginia" command. For purposes of this narrative, all references will be cited as the 1st West Virginia to avoid confusion.
2. "The First's Reunion," *Wheeling Daily Intelligencer*. December 15, 1884.
3. Joseph Thoburn Journal in possession of Suzanne Pezick, Greensboro, North Carolina.
4. Letter of Joseph Thoburn, June 12, 1852, Thomas Thoburn Collection.
5. Joseph Thoburn Journal, Suzanne Pezick Collection.
6. Ibid.
7. Letter of Joseph Thoburn, September 28, 1852, Thomas Thoburn Collection.
8. Joseph Thoburn Journal, Suzanne Pezick Collection.
9. *Wheeling Daily Intelligencer*, July 18, 1865.

10. *Wheeling Daily Intelligencer*, October 26, 1864.
11. Thoburn and his wife Catherine had two children, a six year old boy Martin, and a four year old girl, Mary. *Wheeling Daily Intelligencer*, October 24, 1864; J. H. Newton, G. G. Nichols and A. G. Sprankle, *History of the Pan-Handle; Being Historical Collections of the Counties of Ohio, Brooke, Marshall and Hancock, West Virginia*. (Wheeling: L.A. Caldwell, 1879), p. 253.
12. Joseph Thoburn Journal, Suzanne Pezick Collection.
13. This regiment would officially become the 1st West Virginia Regiment when West Virginia separated from Virginia and achieved statehood in 1863. It will be referred to as the 1st West Virginia from here on out in the text.
14. This quote is from an 1861 edition of the *Wheeling Daily Intelligencer* and was quoted in a modern issue. *Wheeling Daily Intelligencer*, June 19, 2017.
15. C. Stanley Thoburn, *The Ancestry Of The Irish-American Thoburns*. (Cleveland, Ohio, 1955), p. 87.
16. During the Civil War, the term "western" states generally referred to what modern day Americans refer to as the Midwest.
17. Letter from One of Our 1st Virginia Boys," March 29, 1862, *Wheeling Daily Intelligencer*, April 4, 1862.
18. "Colonel Joseph Thoburn," *Wheeling Daily Intelligencer*, March 29, 1862; Letter from One of Our 1st Virginia Boys," March 29, 1862, *Wheeling Daily Intelligencer*, April 4, 1862.
19. Col. E. B. Tyler to Col. Joseph Thoburn, April 7, 1862, *Wheeling Daily Intelligencer*, April 15, 1862.
20. Thoburn's Pledge to Kate Mitchell, Suzanne Pezick Collection; *Wheeling Daily Intelligencer*, April 2 and 8, 1862, July 18, 1865, and October 24 and 26 1864; Newton, p. 253.
21. "From the First Virginia," *Wheeling Daily Intelligencer*, June 16, 1862.
22. Henry J. Johnson to Father, June 11, 1862, contained in *Wheeling Daily Intelligencer*, June 23, 1862; James McElroy, "The Battle of Port Republic as I Saw It."
23. John V. Hadley to Miss Mollie J. Hill, September 16, 1862, *Indiana Magazine of History*, Volume 59, Issue 3, pp. 189-288.
24. John V. Hadley to Miss Mollie J. Hill, September 16, 1862, *Indiana Magazine of History*, Volume 59, Issue 3, pp. 189-288; "Letter from Alexandria," September 3, 1862, *Wheeling Daily Intelligencer*,

September 9, 1862.
25. "The First Virginia Regiment," *Wheeling Daily Intelligencer*, October 14, 1862; "Colonel Thoburn at Home," *Wheeling Daily Intelligencer*, October 22, 1862 and December 17, 1862.
26. Correspondence of Benjamin F. Kelley to the U.S. War Department, January 1864, National Archives.
27. *Wheeling Daily Intelligencer*, February 22, 1864 and March 14, 1864.
28. *Wheeling Daily Intelligencer*, October 24, 1864.

Foreword

29. The Bishop may be forgiven for his error as Hayes and McKinley served in Col. Isaac Duval's division and were, therefore, not directly under Col. Thoburn's command. James M. Thoburn, "Autobiography of James M. Thoburn," *Western Christian Advocate*. April 1911.

Chapter 1

30. See Charles R. Knight's *Valley of Thunder: The Battle of New Market* for a detailed account of the battle and Sigel's campaign.
31. Gov. Arthur I. Boreman was the first governor of West Virginia. Thomas C. Thoburn rose to the rank of 2nd lieutenant in the 50th Ohio Infantry, serving in Gen. William T. Sherman's 1864 Atlanta Campaign. In 1865, he subsequently served as major in the 196th Ohio Infantry. David Thoburn was a newspaper editor of the B*elmont Chronicle* in St. Clairsville, Ohio. Captain J. M. Doudy is likely John Dowdy of the 3rd West Virginia Cavalry.
32. Captain John McNeil's Rangers raided Piedmont in Mineral County, West Virginia, an important stop on the Baltimore and Ohio Railroad. This raid disrupted Maj. Gen. Franz Sigel's campaign in the Shenandoah Valley. This is not to be confused with the subsequent battle of Piedmont, in Augusta County, Virginia.
33. The *Baltimore American* is a Newspaper.
34. The cavalry of Brig. Gen. John D. Imboden opposed Sigel's advance. Brig. Gen. Thomas Rosser was with the Army of Northern Virginia and was not in the Shenandoah Valley.

35. In the Shenandoah Valley, moving down the Valley means moving northward and up the Valley means moving southward. The up and down terminology follows the flow of the Shenandoah River which flows generally northward to Harpers Ferry where it joins the Potomac River.
36. Battery D, 1st West Virginia Light Artillery.
37. Battle of Spotsylvania, May 12, 1864.
38. Major General Governeur K. Warren commander of the Army of the Potomac's Fifth Corps was not killed in the fighting between Grant and Lee. This is an example of the rampant nature of the army's rumor mill.
39. Colonel Augustus Moor of the 28th Ohio.
40. Col. George D. Wells of the 34th Massachusetts reported, "Colonel Thoburn, commander of the brigade, rode along the lines telling the men to 'prepare to charge.' He rode by me shouting some order I could not catch, and went to the regiment on my left [the 1st West Virginia] which immediately charged. I supposed this to be his order to me, and I commanded to fix bayonets and charge. The men fairly sprang forward."
41. Thoburn is referring to Grant's attack on the Confederate position at Spotsylvania on May 12 that captured thousands of prisoners and many cannon, but did not succeed in breaking Lee's army.
42. These entrenchments were constructed on a commanding hill overlooking the town by General Nathaniel Banks during the 1862 Valley Campaign and subsequently became known as Bank's Fort.
43. The field officer of the day is responsible for overall security of the army. Thoburn had to ensure that pickets or guards were properly posted to prevent surprise attacks or unauthorized personnel from entering the Union lines.

Chapter 2

44. OR, 37:1:517-518.

Headquarters Department of West Virginia,
In the Field, Near Cedar Creek
May, 22, 1864

General Orders No. 29

It is of the utmost importance that this army be placed in a situation for immediate efficiency. We are contending against an enemy who is in earnest, and, if we expect success, we, too, must be in earnest. We must be willing to make sacrifices, willing to suffer for a short time, that a glorious result may crown our efforts.

The country is expecting every man to do his duty; and this done, an ever kind Providence will certainly grant us complete success.

I. Every tent will be immediately turned in, for transportation to Martinsburg; and all baggage not expressly allowed by this order, will be at once sent to the rear. There will be but one wagon allowed to each Regiment, and this will only be used to transport spare ammunition, camp kettles, tools and mess-pans Every wagon will have eight picket horses, two drivers, and two saddles. One wagon and one ambulance will be allowed to Department Headquarters, and the same to Division and Brigade Headquarters. The other ambulances will be under the immediate order of the Medical Director.

II. For the expedition on hand, the clothes each soldier has on his back, with one pair of extra shoes and socks, are amply sufficient. Everything else in the shape of clothing will be packed today and shipped to the rear. Each knapsack will contain one hundred rounds of ammunition, carefully packed; four pounds of hard bread to last eight days; ten rations of coffee, sugar and salt, one pair of shoes and socks, and nothing else.

III. Brigade and all other Commanders will be held strictly responsible that their commands are supplied from the country. Cattle, sheep, and hogs, and if necessary, horses and mules must be taken, and slaughtered. These supplies will be seized under the direction of officers duly authorized, and upon a system which will hereafter be regulated. No straggling or pillaging will be allowed. Brigade and other Commanders will be held responsible that there is no waste; and that there is a proper and orderly division amongst their men, of the supplies taken for our use.

IV. Commanders will attend personally to the prompt execution of this order, so that we may move to-morrow morning. They will see that in passing through a country in this way, depending upon it for forage and supplies, great additional vigilance is required on the part of every officer in the command of men, for the enforcement of discipline.

V. The Commanding General expects from every officer and soldier of the army in the field, an earnest and unhesitating support; and relies with confidence upon an ever kind Providence for the result. The Lieutenant General commanding the armies of the United States, who is now victoriously pressing back the enemy, upon their last stronghold, expects much from the Army of the Shenandoah; and he must not be disappointed.

VI. In conclusion, the Major General commanding, while holding every officer to the strictest responsibility of his position, and prepared to enforce discipline, with severity, when necessary, will never cease to urge the prompt promotion of all officers, non commissioned officers, and enlisted men, who earn recognition by their gallantry and good conduct.

> By command of
> Major General Hunter
> Chas. G. Halpine
> Assistant Adjutant General

45. Confederate General Tom Rosser was not in the Valley. The cavalry in questions belonged to Brig. Gen. John D. Imboden. Maj. Gen.

George Crook had raided into Southwest Virginia in early May of 1864. He won a victory of Confederate Gen. Alfred G. Jenkins at the Battle of Cloyd's Mountain on May 9 and burned the vital Virginia and Tennessee Railroad bridge over the New River near modern day Radford, Virginia. Crook then fell back to the vicinity of Lewisburg, West Virginia where he received orders from Hunter to join his force at Staunton. Thoburn had a correct understanding of the situation.

46. Thoburn's words proved prophetic. Hunter's burnings as well as Maj. Gen. Philip H. Sheridan's general burning of Valley farms, crops and resources in the fall of 1864, continued to be a source of much resentment among Shenandoah natives even into the 21st Century 150 years after the war ended.

47. Major Harry Gilmor commanded the 2nd Maryland Cavalry Battalion. During this campaign, it operated as partisan rangers in the Shendandoah Valley, attacking Hunter's supply trains as they ventured up the Valley to reinforce the Army of the Shenandoah. Capt. Hanse McNeil led a Ranger Company out of the South Branch Valley in West Virginia that operated in the Valley at this time conducting scouting duty.

48. Breckinridge was with Lee and the Army of Northern Virginia at Cold Harbor outside of Richmond. Crook was moving toward Buffalo Gap, but was only opposed by a small force of Confederate cavalry under the command of Col. William L. "Mudwall" Jackson.

49. Col. Algernon Gray had opposed secession in 1861, and in 1864 he offered his home to General Hunter to use as his headquarters while in Harrisonburg. After Hunter's army left the area citizens threatened the Gray family with death, Algernon and his brother Robert fled to Baltimore. Jed Hotchkiss to Wife, July 3, 1864, Library of Congress.

50. Maj. Gen. Nathaniel Banks failed Red River Campaign and harrowing retreat in Louisiana led Thoburn to except that from the general forward movement of Union armies across the South.

51. In Louisiana, Thoburn's former commander, General Banks, was defeated in the Red River Campaign and forced to abandon his advance.

52. Two companies of "Boys" and a company of "Old Men" took part in the Battle of Piedmont as well as reserves from Rockingham,

Augusta and Rockbridge Counties. Also, some of these men were captured and wounded and expressed their support for the Union and told of being impressed into the Confederate ranks against their will.

53. Confederate Gen. John D. Imboden had earlier proposed just that plan to Gen. William E. Jones who was leading reinforcements to the Valley from Southwest Virginia and East Tennessee. Thoburn led the 1st West Virginia Infantry in the Battle of Port Republic on June 9, 1862, as a part of Major General James Shields' division. After holding off Jackson's superior force and inflicting heavy losses upon the Southerners, the Union force was forced to retreat toward Luray.
54. The 31st Virginia was not at Piedmont. C. J. Rawling, historian of the 1st West Virginia, identified the captured flag as belonging to the 36th Virginia. This regiment was heavily engaged at Piedmont and fought opposite the 1st West Virginia.
55. Hunter would have about 16,000 men once he joined forces with Crook. Crook commanded an infantry division and Averell a cavalry division.
56. Col. William L. "Mudwall" Jackson led a force of about 900 men to resist Crook's 8,000 man force through the Mountains. Crook noted that "Mudwall" received his nickname in "contradistinction" to his legendary cousin Stonewall Jackson. The engagement Thoburn wrote of occurred at Panther Gap and was a small skirmish where Crook easily flanked the Confederates out of their position. Crook also destroyed the Virginia Central Railroad as he approached Staunton from the west.
57. Johnston proved unable to stop Sherman in Georgia.
58. Lee repulsed Grant's attacks in a bloody battle at Cold Harbor on June 3, but Grant maintained his position.
59. Confederate Gen. John D. Imboden's cavalry prevented Col. William B. Tibbitts's cavalry from reaching Waynesboro. Tibbitts destroyed the Virginia Central Railroad east of Staunton but was prevented from getting to Waynesboro. Beyond Waynesboro, the railroad passed through the mountains via Blue Ridge Tunnel which was guarded by Breckinridge who had returned to the Valley after the debacle at Piedmont. Breckinridge had three infantry brigades and four batteries to defend the tunnel. While he was outnumbered

by Hunter, his force was substantial enough to utilize the terrain and prevent Hunter from moving directly over the Blue Ridge to Charlottesville.

Chapter 3

60. Midway, Virginia is now named Steele's Tavern.
61. Brig. Gen. Alfred Duffie's cavalry division moved to cut the Orange and Alexandria Railroad between Lynchburg and Charlottesville. Duffie had taken command of Maj. Gen. Julius Stahel's division. The latter had been wounded at Piedmont. Duffie had previously commanded a brigade under Averell and had only been with Hunter's army for a few days, likely leading Thoburn to assume that the railroad raiders were part of Averell's division.
62. McCausland had recently been promoted to brigadier general and placed in command of the deceased Albert G. Jenkins cavalry brigade. Previously, McCausland had commanded the 36th Virginia Infantry. This may have led to confusion on the composition of his force at Lexington, but the Confederate commanded a brigade of cavalry supported by a battery of artillery.
63. Contrary to the rumor Thoburn reported, Gen. George Pickett's division did not move to the Shenandoah Valley or Lynchburg.
64. Liberty is now the town of Bedford.
65. East of modern day Roanoke, Virginia.
66. This engagement is known as the battle of Hanging Rock, Roanoke County, Virginia.
67. Sweet Spring was a Sulphur spring resort reputed to have healing qualities like many similar places frequented in that era. It is located in Monroe County, West Virginia.
68. Hawk's Nest is now a West Virginia State Park located in Ansted.
69. When Hunter withdrew into the mountains of West Virginia, Jubal Early led his force down the Shenandoah Valley and invaded Maryland, occupying Martinsburg before crossing the Potomac River.

Chapter 4

70. Henry Kyd Douglas, *I Rode with Stonewall*, p. 284.
71. Sullivan had consistently underperformed throughout the 1864 campaign dating back to the Battle of New Market. Only the lack of viable brigadier generals kept him in his position as long as he lasted. Crook decided to go with the reliable Thoburn even though he lacked the star most division commanders wore.
72. Piedmont, not to be confused with the village in the Shenandoah where Thoburn fought on June 5, is located in Mineral County, West Virginia, on the south bank of the North Branch of the Potomac River. It is roughly 27 miles south of Frostburg, Maryland, the most substantial nearby town.
73. "Lots of Used Up Boys," *Wheeling Daily Intelligencer*, July 8, 1864.
74. Green Spring Creek flows into the Potomac River. It also gives its name to a railroad stop on the B & O Railroad opposite of Oldtown, Maryland.
75. Cherry Run is another stop in West Virginia along the railroad, southeast of Hancock, Maryland.
76. Thomas C. Thoburn, *My Experiences During the Civil War*. Appendix B, 5.
77. Hedgesville is located just west of Martinsburg on the railroad.
78. Confederate Brigadier General William C. Vaughn.
79. General Albion P. Howe. Early was actually marching toward Washington, D.C.
80. Col. Robert M. Richardson was commander of the 15th New York Cavalry. He eventually resigned his command on January 17, 1865.
81. In addition to the Sixth Corps from the Army of the Potomac, Grant diverted the Nineteenth Corps which had just arrived at City Point near Petersburg from New Orleans to Washington to resist Early. Many of the Nineteenth Corps troops never disembarked from the steamers at City Point, but the ships were diverted to Washington.
82. Weverton, Maryland, is located on the Potomac River about three miles east of Harper's Ferry.
83. Col. Samuel Baldwin Marks Young was from the 4th Pennsylvania Cavalry. His command was made up of dismounted men from nearly every cavalry regiment in the Army of the Potomac. It lacked

in unit cohesion and did not perform well, although Young was credited for his bravery.
84. Thoburn was correct and Baguley mustered out at the end of his term of service in November 1864.
85. The cannon fire heard by Thoburn was from the Union horse artillery shelling Early's withdrawing rear guard in Loudoun County from across the Potomac River near Edward's Ferry.
86. Ironcially, Crook recognized Mulligan's shortcomings and permitted Thoburn to remain in command of the division for the rest of the 1864 Campaign. Mulligan was given a small, ad-hoc division so as to not disrupt continuity of command that Thoburn had gained with his troops through the 1864 Valley Campaign. Mulligan noted his dissatisfaction with Crook, noting that Crook's name reflected the nature of his actions.
87. Asa Janney must have done a good job selling himself as a loyal Unionist. He had voted for secession in 1861, and his son joined the 8th Virginia Infantry and lost a leg at Bull Run in 1861. Perhaps his views had changed after witnessing the devastating injury to his son and three years of hardship brought on by the war, but most likely, he said what he needed to convince the Union officers of his loyalty and avoid any confrontation. Richard Gillespie, "The Civil War Comes Home to Roost," *The Thomas Balch Chronicle*, Summer 2014.
88. Long was Early's chief of artillery.
89. Only five companies of the 123rd Ohio moved from the extreme right. This regiments filled a gap on the right center of the breaking line, while the 116th Ohio continued to the extreme left and stemmed the tide in that sector. *Wyandot Pioneer*, July 29, 1864.
90. U. S. losses at Snickers Gap or Cool Spring were actually 65 killed, 301 wounded and 56 missing, many of whom were drowned. Confederate losses exceeded 300. The battle was termed a "right smart little fight" by one of Thoburn's West Virginians.
91. The artillery fire Thoburn heard was actually farther to the west from the area north of Winchester from combat by Brig. Gen. William W. Averell's division as it marched on Winchester from Bunker Hill, West Virginia.
92. The artillery fire on the evening of July 19 was from Brig. Gen. Alfred Duffie's Cavalry failing in its effort to cross the Shenandoah River at Berry's Ferry after passing through Ashby's Gap. Duffie was

attempting to get around Early's southern flank at the time.
93. Murray was not killed but survived his wound but was captured by the Confederates.
94. Hoge was an acquaintance of the Thoburn clan from the St. Clairsville, Ohio, area.

Chapter 5

95. Patchan, 153, 159.
96. R. E. Lee to Jefferson Davis, July 23, 1864, OR, 37:1:346 and 2:599.
97. This would be former Vice-President of the United States and 1861 Southern Democratic Presidential candidate John C. Breckinridge of Kentucky, and Maj. Gen. Robert E. Rodes of Lynchburg, Virginia.
98. Confederate losses were not as high as Thoburn related and likely did not exceed 400 total casualties.
99. The Lincoln Administration had placed Crook in command of Hunter's Army. Hunter remained the departmental commander, but Crook was given command of the field army.
100. The newspaper likely told of Sherman's victory at the battle of Peachtree Creek on July 20.
101. Thoburn's brigades found Confederate Maj. Gen. Stephen D. Ramseur's division and Col. William L. "Mudwall" Jackson's cavalry brigade firmly blocking Thoburn's planned avenue of advance. In addition to Mulligan, Col. Rutherford B. Hayes' brigade was routed on the left.
102. The Confederate Army of the Valley District, like all elements of Gen. Robert E. Lee's Army of Northern Virginia, had a formally established sharpshooter corps. Jubal Early made excellent use of his sharpshooters, their effectiveness as measured by the heavy casualties they inflicted, often convinced the Union forces that they were matched against a larger force than they actually were. Kernstown and Snickers Gap are two prime examples.
103. Ganotown is an unincorporated hamlet located approximately ten miles west of modern day Inwood, West Virginia.
104. Shanghai is a hamlet in the Back Creek Valley.
105. The Back Creek Valley runs parallel to the Valley Pike west of

North Mountain and about six miles west of the pike. Sleepy Creek and Cherry Run are stops on the Baltimore and Ohio Railroad west of Martinsburg. Capt. Petrie had fortified a steam engine and some cars with steel plating and created an armored train that was used to defend the B & O Railroad.

106. Brig. Gen. Averell commanded a cavalry division in Crook's army.

Chapter 6

107. Achilles Tynes, "Notes on the Battlefield and in the Saddle, for Hattie," Achilles Tynes Papers, Duke University; Patchan, *Shenandoah Summer*, 271-290.
108. *New York Times*, July 11, 1864; OR 37:2:426.
109. Capt. Robert S. Gardner was a quartermaster who had originally served in the 23rd Ohio Infantry but was transferred to the U.S. Volunteers Quartermaster's Department in 1862.
110. Thoburn's statement about the severity of the 1864 Valley Campaign is significant given that he participated in the arduous campaign against Stonewall Jackson in the Valley in 1862 and against Robert E. Lee in August of 1862, fighting and marching from Cedar Mountain through the Second Battle of Manassas under extremely dire circumstances.
111. This was the Battle of the Crater. The assault began successfully but turned into an embarrassing fiasco with heavy losses among Union troops and all gains were lost by the day's end.
112. Thoburn remained in command of his division until his death at Cedar Creek on October 19, 1864. Sullivan was sent to Charleston, West Virginia, to assume command of the U.S. forces in the Kanawha Valley. OR 45:1;709, 749.
113. Jacob Miller Campbell mustered out of service on September 3, 1864. Harris took over command of his brigade. Ely's 18th Connecticut was assigned garrison duty in early September, and he no longer commanded a brigade.
114. The Confederate movements did not constitute another invasion of Maryland/Pennsylvania. Jubal Early had launched some diversionary maneuvers. The Second Corps, Army of the Potomac did not join Union forces in the Valley. However, Sheridan and two

cavalry divisions form that army soon joined the U.S. Forces in the Valley.

Prologue

115. Mr. Hornbrook is the father of Lt. Henry Hornbrook, 1st West Virginia Infantry.
116. Grant had no intention of relieving Hunter but intended that he exercise department command and Sheridan would be in charge of the field army in the Valley. However, Hunter recognized the situation as inserting another layer of bureaucracy into the command structure and stepped aside as a matter of practicality, earning Grant's praise for his patriotism.
117. Mary Thoburn was Joseph's sister who was engaged to be married.
118. "Sis" is another of Joseph's five sisters. It is likely either Isabell or Eliza Ann, his youngest siblings. Isabella became a missionary and never married.
119. Thoburn's preferred suitor was Captain George B. Macomber of the 34th Massachusetts. Macomber remained in the army after the war and was accidentally killed in 1869 by a falling derrick.
120. The net worth was not located on the document.
121. John G. Farrar, "Personal Account of the Civil War," February 14, 1895 at http://www.civil-war.net/users/john_farrar/john_farrar.asp on July 17, 2016.
122. William Dwight, Report of Service, National Archives.
123. The staff officers are Lt. Federick L. Ballard, 116th Ohio, Lt. George B. Macomber, 34th Masschusetts (Acting Assistant Inspector General); Lt. Henry H. Hornbook, 1st West Virginia (Aid-de-camp and Quartermaster); and Lt. Samuel A. Rollyson, 10th West Virginia.
124. OR, 43:1:368-369.
125. Private John Creed of the 23rd Illinois and Private George G. Moore of the 11th West Virginia captured the battle flags mentioned by Thoburn. OR, 43:1:369-371.
126. OR 43:1:50 and 43:2:249.
127. Joseph Wheelan, *Terrible Swift Sword: The Life General Philip H. Sheridan*. 130.
128. Former commander of the Army of the Potomac had challenged

Abraham Lincoln as the Democratic candidate in the 1864 election on a platform that would end the war and essentially grant the South independence. McClellanism was a reference to his supporters and platform.
129. The officers referenced were likely Brig. Gen. John D. Stevenson, Brig. Gen. Joseph A. J. Lightburn, and Brig. Gen. Max von Weber.
130. C. Stanley Thoburn, 88-89.
131. Wildes' and Karr's accounts of the early morning occurrences in Thoburn's camp agree in all respects but one. Karr identifies the division commander as Col. Harris. Both men state that Karr was sent to see the DIVISION COMMANDER, so this author has concluded that Karr mistakenly placed Harris in command of the division at that time. Harris would become the division commander upon the mortal wounding of Thoburn a short while later, so it is easy to see Karr confusing the two men in the intervening 45 years. OR, 43:1:379,382; Thomas F. Wildes, Record of the 116th Ohio Infantry Volunteers, 202-203; *National Tribune*, October 14, 1909.
132. *Wheeling Daily Intelligencer*, October 26, 1864.
133. Charles Lynch, *The Civil War Diary of Charles H. Lynch, 18th Connecticut Volunteers*. Hartford: 1915, p. 130.
134. *Wheeling Daily Intelligencer*, October 22, 1864.
135. Ely served with Thoburn in the 1864 Valley Campaign, most of the time as a regimental commander of the 18th Connecticut during the Lynchburg Campaign and then as a brigade commander when Thoburn rose to division command.
136. Samuel Heintzelman Journal, Library of Congress.
137. Catherine Thoburn, contained in Col. Thoburn's Journal, in possession of Suzanne Pezick, Greensboro, North Carolina.

Appendix A

138. Tyler's brigade marched from east to west to get into position to attack the Southern forces with the skirmish companies deployed between the marching column and the Confederate position. When the column turned leftward to approach the enemy position which was not known with certainty at the time, the skirmishers were in front of the advancing column.

139. Duval left the 1st Virginia after the Battle of Port Republic and became colonel of the 9th Virginia Infantry, U.S. Duval would serve side-by-side with Thoburn as a fellow brigade and division commander during the 1864 Shenandoah Valley campaign, until Duval was wounded at the Battle of Opequon Creek, or Third Winchester, on September 19.
140. Conrad's Store is now called Elkton.
141. Jackson's force numbered about 15,000.
142. In general, the Army of Northern Virginia was at its strongest point in terms of manpower during the Seven Days Battles which Thoburn refers to as the "late 8 days fighting." Stephen W. Sears places Gen. Robert E. Lee's strengths at just over 92,000 men on the eve of those battles. McClellan's Army of the Potomac numbered nearly 106,000 at the same time. Sears, To the Gates of Richmond: The Peninsula Campaign. (New York: Tichnor and Fields, 1992), 156-7.

Appendix B

143. West Virginia State Archives, Charleston, WV.
144. The flag captured actually belonged to the 36th Virginia Infantry.

Appendix C

145. *Wheeling Daily Intelligencer*, October 26, 1864.
146. *Wheeling Weekly Register*, November 10, 1864.

Index

Adams, John 123
Alex, Dr. 126
Alexandria, Virginia 16, 17, 124
Alleghany Mountains 13
Anderson, Richard H. 96, 97
Annapolis, Maryland 61
Antietam Battlefield 86
Army of Northern Virginia 15, 21, 45, 71, 72, 96, 98
Army of the Potomac 14, 21, 24, 30, 45, 68, 82, 89, 90, 92, 110
Army of the Rappahannock 12
Army of the Shenandoah 33, 87, 96, 98, 105, 107
Army of the Valley District 71, 105
Army of Virginia 14
Army of West Virginia 20, 71, 96, 97, 99, 102, 103, 105
Ashby's Gap, Virginia 68
Atlanta, Georgia 23, 60, 73, 105
Averell, William Woods 41, 42, 47, 48, 49, 73, 77, 82

Back Creek 60, 77
Baguley, David 63, 94
Baker, Lt. 94
Ballard, Frederick L. 94, 101
Baltimore American 24, 25, 26, 35, 82, 104
Baltimore and Ohio Railroad 9, 11, 17, 35, 55, 57, 58, 107
Baltimore, Maryland 61, 91
Banks, Nathaniel 12, 14

Barbour Creek 53
Bates, Dr. 126
Beauregard, Pierre G.T. 26
Bedford County, Virginia 49
Belle Grove plantation 22
Belleville, Maryland 80
Belmont County, Ohio 3, 68, 107, 111
Berlin, (Brunswick) Maryland 63
Berryville, Battle of 97, 110
Berryville Road 66
Berryville, Virginia 95
Beverly, West Virginia 46
Bier, Philip 101, 103, 104, 110, 114, 115
Big Sewell Mountain 54
Blue Ridge Mountains 12, 13, 14, 43, 45, 47, 48, 97, 105
Blue's Gap, Battle of 11
Bolivar Heights, West Virginia 91
Bonsack Station, Virginia 52
Boreman, Arthur I. 23, 107
Breckinridge, John C. 21, 26, 33, 37, 45, 51, 72
Brinniman, Lt. 94
Brown's Gap 105
Brownsburg, Virginia 47
Brownsville, Pennsylvania 4
Buchanan, James 21
Buchanan, Virginia 45, 48
Buffalo Gap, Virginia 37, 42
Bull Run 16
Bull Run, First Battle of (see also Manassas) 8, 121

Bull Run, Second Battle of (see also Manassas) 15, 16
Bunker Hill, West Virginia 76, 77
Burkittsville, Maryland 80
Butler, Benjamin 25, 26

Caball, James 123
Callendilne, Samuel 123
Camp Piatt 55
Campbell, Jacob M. 84, 85, 128
Carmack, Stockton 68, 83, 110
Carrickfergus, Northern Ireland 3
Carroll, Samuel S. 14, 15, 121
Castleman's Ferry, Virginia 72
Catawba Mountains 52
Catlett Station, Virginia 12
Catoctin Mountain 82
Cedar Creek, Virginia 22, 25, 30, 34, 35, 96, 107
Cedar Creek, Battle of 18, 110, 114
Cedar Mountain, Battle of 14
Centre Wheeling Station 11
Chamberlain, Benjamin F. 121-2
Chambersburg, Pennsylvania 79, 82, 89
Charles Town, West Virginia 67, 86, 97
Charleston, West Virginia 57
Charlottesville, Virginia 47, 79
Cherry Run, West Virginia 59, 60, 61, 77
Cleveland, Ohio 124
Clouds Mill, Virginia 124
Cloyd's Mountain, Battle of 84

Cold Harbor, Battle of 42
Columbia Furnace, Virginia 26
Columbus, Ohio 4, 5
Connecticut units
  18th Connecticut Infantry 50
Conrad's Store (Elkton), Virginia 121
Cool Spring, Battle of (also Snickers Ferry/Ford/Gap, Island Ford, or Castleman's Ferry) 62, 64, 65
Cowen, Benjamin Rush 113
Cowen, Ellen (Thoburn) 113
Craig County, Virginia 53
Crapo, Angelo 84
Crater, Battle of the 79, 82
Crook, George 35, 37, 38, 39, 41, 42, 45, 47, 49, 52, 54, 58, 65, 66, 67, 68, 71, 73, 75, 79, 80, 82, 84, 85, 91, 92, 95, 97, 99, 102, 103, 104, 106, 107, 114
Cross Keys, Battle of 13
Culpeper, Virginia 14
Cumberland, Maryland 17, 61
Curtis, William B. 76, 78, 127, 128
Cutshaw, Wilfred E. 105

Daily Intelligencer 115, 119, 121
Dalton, Georgia 24
Dayton, J.H. 127
Dayton, Virginia 104
Desal, Gertrude ("Getty") 5
Dickey, Mr. 93
Doudy, J.M. 23
Drummond, Rev. Dr. 110
Duffie, Alfred 47, 52, 82

INDEX 155

DuPont, Henry A. 128
Duval, Isaac H. 73, 76, 84, 97, 99, 100, 120, 123

Early, Jubal A. 45, 49, 50, 51, 57, 58, 61, 67, 71, 79, 83, 96, 97, 98, 105, 107
Edie, John 123
Edward's Ferry, Maryland 61
Ely, William G. 76, 84, 110
Emory, William H. 97, 100
Ewell, Richard S. 60
Ewing, James M. 101

Fisher's Hill, Battle of 102, 105
Fisher's Hill, Virginia 30, 71, 96, 98, 99
Frank Leslie's Illustrated Newspaper 104
Frederick County, Virginia 112, 131
Frederick, Maryland 61, 79, 82, 83, 86
Frederick Pike 61
Fredericksburg, Virginia 13
Fremont, John C. 13, 123
Front Royal, Virginia 14
Frost, Daniel 68, 69

Ganotown, West Virginia 77
Gardner, Robert S. 80, 81
Gauley River 54
Germantown, Pennsylvania 3
Gilmor, Harry 37
Gordonsville, Virginia 45, 79
Grafton, West Virginia 34

Grant, Ulysses S. 18, 21, 22, 24, 25, 26, 30, 33, 37, 38, 42, 45, 47, 48, 54, 57, 60, 61, 72, 79, 80, 82, 86, 89, 96, 105
Gray, Algeron 38
Greeley, Horace 75
Green Spring River 59
Greenville, Virginia 46

Hagerstown, Maryland 77, 78, 82
Halleck, Henry 79, 80
Halltown, West Virginia 67, 80, 86, 91, 96, 97
Halstead, Joseph 44
Hancock County, West Virginia 123
Harper's Ferry, West Virginia 58, 61, 63, 65, 67, 85, 86, 91, 96, 107
Harris, Thomas M. 84, 99, 100, 101, 102
Harrisonburg, Virginia 12, 13, 37, 38, 39, 104, 105, 106
Hawk's Nest, West Virginia (see also Marshall's Pillars) 54
Hayes, Rutherford B. 19, 20, 99
Hedgesville, West Virginia 61
Heintzleman, Samuel 110
Herrick, Major 94
Hill, Ambrose Powell 15
Hillsboro, Virginia 58, 63, 65
Hoge, George W. 68
Honeyville, Virginia 121
Hoover, Mary E. 108, 131, 132
Hornbrook, Henry H. 94, 101
Hornbrook, Mr. 91, 93

Howe, Albion P. 61
Hunter, David 33, 34, 35, 36, 37, 39, 45, 46, 48, 49, 50, 51, 53, 57, 58, 60, 65, 67, 80, 83, 84, 86, 89, 90, 91, 95, 105, 128

Imboden, John D. 25, 37, 42, 59, 61
Indiana units
  7th Indiana Infantry 120, 122, 123
  14th Indiana Infantry 120
Irwin, David 38

Jackson, Thomas J. "Stonewall" 11, 12, 13, 14, 15, 45, 71, 119, 121, 122, 123
Jackson, William Lowther "Mudwall" 42
James River 24, 25, 47, 48
Janney, Asa 65
Jenkins, Benjamin 110, 115
Johnson, Henry J. 123
Johnston, Joseph E. 42
Jones, William E. "Grumble" 33, 128

Kanawha Falls 54, 55
Kanawha River 54, 55, 57, 60, 67
Karr, Hamilton L. 108
Kearneysville, West Virginia 63
Kelley, Benjamin F. 8, 9, 11, 17, 110
Kernstown, First Battle of 11, 13, 119
Kernstown, Second Battle of 72, 74, 79

Kernstown, Virginia 25
Kerr, Daniel 123
Kershaw, Joseph B. 97, 105
Kimball, Nathan 11
King Charles I 3
Kirby, Charles W. 101
Knoxville, Maryland 80

Lander, Frederick W. 9, 11
Lacey Springs, Virginia 37
Lee, Robert E. 14, 15, 21, 22, 25, 26, 30, 33, 35, 38, 42, 45, 57, 60, 71, 72, 91, 96
Leesburg, Virginia 63, 65
Lester McCombs 55
Letcher, John 47
Lewisburg, West Virginia 53
Lexington, Virginia 45, 47, 48, 49
Liberty, (Bedford) Virginia 48, 49, 50, 51, 52
Lincoln, Abraham 14, 18, 21, 26, 57, 79, 80, 97, 98
Little Catawba Creek 52
Little North Mountain 99, 102
Little Mountain 53
Long, Armistead L. 66
Loudon County, Virginia 58, 63, 83, 97
Lovettsville, Virginia 63
Luray Valley 13, 14
Luray, Virginia 121
Lynch, Charles 110
Lynchburg, Virginia 30, 45, 47, 48, 49, 50, 57, 60, 95

Macomber, George S. 94, 101

Manassas, First Battle of (see also Bull Run) 8, 121
Manassas, Second Battle of (see also Bull Run) 15, 16
Manassas, Virginia 124
Mannis Creek 54
Marshall's Pillars 54
Martinsburg, West Virginia 23, 25, 34, 37, 55, 57, 59, 61, 63, 67, 76, 77
Maryland units
　2nd Maryland Potomac Home Brigade 61
　2nd Maryland Eastern Shore 61, 127, 128
Massachusetts units
　34th Massachusetts Infantry 21, 26, 29, 99, 101, 127, 128
Massanutten Mountain 13, 108
McCausland, John 47, 48, 82
McClellan, George B. 12, 13, 14, 48, 124, 125
McCollum, Charles B. 101
McDowell, Irvin 12, 13
McIlwain, Lt. 84, 94
McKinley, William 19, 20, 104
McNeill, John Hanson 37
McPhail, Daniel H. 110
Meadow Bluff, West Virginia 54
Meigs, John R. 104
Merryman, Thomas 123
Middle Mountain 53
Middletown, Maryland 80
Middletown, Virginia 22, 108, 131, 132
Midway, Virginia 46, 47
Milroy, Robert 72

Miss Hales 54
Mobile, Alabama 92
Moffat, Rev. Mr. 110
Monocacy, Battle of 57
Monocacy Junction, Maryland 83
Monocacy River 83
Moor, Augustus 27, 29
Moorefield, West Virginia 17
Morgan, Captain 106
Morris, Thomas 68
Mosby, John Singleton 25
Mount Jackson, Virginia 26, 27
Mount Pleasant, Ohio 111, 124
Mount Wood Cemetery 111, 116
Mulligan, James A. 65, 73, 75, 76, 78
Murray, Edward 68

Naked Creek 121
Napoleon 125
Natural Bridge, Virginia 48
New Castle, Virginia 52, 53
New London, Virginia 49
New Market, Battle of 2, 18, 21-2, 28, 31, 33, 60, 110
New Market, Virginia 27, 36, 37, 39
New River 54
New York Times 79
New York units
　5th New York Heavy Artillery 68
　15th New York Cavalry 30, 61
　21st New York Cavalry 30
Newtown, Virginia 37

Noland, Joseph 123
North Mountain 52, 77
Nugent, James 78

Ohio 3, 4
Ohio County, West Virginia 18
Ohio River 3, 5, 57, 111
Ohio State Lunatic Asylum 4
Ohio units
  5th Ohio Infantry 123
  7th Ohio Infantry 120, 122, 123
  23rd Ohio Infantry 84, 85
  29th Ohio Infantry 13, 120, 122, 123
  50th Ohio Infantry 23, 105
  66th Ohio Infantry 123
  116th Ohio Infantry 67, 68, 108
  123rd Ohio Infantry 67
  126th Ohio Infantry 68
  196th Ohio Infantry 23
Old Sweet Spring, West Virginia 53
Opequon Creek, 97, 99
Opequon Creek, Battle of 2
Orange and Alexandria Railroad 12, 45
Otter Creek 49, 51
Otter River 49

Page County, Virginia 121
Parker's Ford (also Castleman's Ford) 72
Parkersburg, West Virginia 55, 57
Patterson, Samuel S. 84

Peaks of Otter, Virginia 45, 48
Peninsula Campaign 12
Pennsylvania units
  54th Pennsylvania Infantry 21, 29, 127, 128
  84th Pennsylvania Infantry 123
  110th Pennsylvania Infantry 123
Peters Mountain 53
Petersburg, Virginia 26, 45, 57, 61, 72, 80, 82, 92
Petersburg, West Virginia 17
Petersville, Maryland 80
Petrie, Peter B. 77
Pickett, George E. 47
Piedmont, Battle of 2, 22, 33, 39, 40, 41, 127
Piedmont, Virginia 39, 41
Piedmont, West Virginia 24, 58
Philippi, Battle of 8, 9
Pittsylvania mansion 15
Po River 26
Pope, John 14, 15, 16
Port Republic, Battle of 121
Port Republic, Virginia 13, 14, 15, 38, 39, 105, 121
Potomac River 63, 65, 79, 80, 82, 86, 91
Prather, George 123
Purcellville, Virginia 58, 65
Purgatory Mountains 48

Rapidan River 15, 24, 68
Rappahannock River 15
Ravenswood, West Virginia 55
Redbud Run 99, 100

INDEX 159

Reed, Thomas 132, 133
Richardson, Robert M. 61
Richmond, Virginia 12, 14, 26, 33, 35, 37, 38, 45, 51, 71, 72, 82, 105
Rider, James H. 66, 68, 94, 128
Ritchietown, West Virginia 11
Roanoke, Virginia 57
Robinson, Lucius N. 122
Rodes, Robert E. 72
Rodgers, R.S. 127
Rollyson, Samuel A. 101
Rosekrans, Isaac A. 84, 94
Rosser, Thomas L. 25, 35, 105, 107
Round Top Mountain 103
Rude's Hill, Virginia 36, 37

Saint Clairsville, Ohio 124
Salem, Virginia 52, 60
Sandy Hook, Maryland 78, 80, 86, 90
Seven Mile Mountain 53
Shanghai, West Virginia 77
Sharpsburg, Maryland 85
Shelley, Dick 104
Shenandoah River 27, 29, 64, 65, 91, 98-9, 121
Shepherdstown, West Virginia 80
Sheridan, Philip H. 19, 45, 80, 86, 87, 89, 91, 96, 97, 99, 100, 104, 105, 106, 107, 108
Sherman, William T. 23, 24, 26, 42, 54, 60, 73, 90, 93, 105
Shields, James 11, 12, 13, 14, 39, 75, 121

Sigel, Franz 18, 21, 22, 25, 31, 33, 34, 61, 63
Sleepy Creek 77
Snickers Gap, Battle of (see also Cool Spring, Battle of) 2, 62, 65
Snickers Gap, Virginia 65, 66, 71
South Mountain 80
Stahel, Julius 21, 30, 63
Starling Medical School 4
Starr, William C. 104
Staunton, Virginia 33, 35, 37, 39, 41, 42, 45, 46, 47, 92, 106
Steel, Mr. 24
Stephens, Edward W. 58
Stock, Henry 95
Strasburg Road 73
Strasburg, Virginia 22, 23, 25, 27, 30, 34, 68, 96, 98
Strobel, Robert 2
Strong Creek 27
Sullivan, Jeremiah C. 21, 30, 37, 47, 58, 59, 61, 63, 65, 66, 67, 73, 84

Taylor, George 123
Taylor, James E. 104, 109, 112
Thoburn, Anna Lyle 5, 6, 10
Thoburn, David 23, 68, 107
Thoburn, Eliza 113, 126
Thoburn, James M. 19
Thoburn, Jennie 7
Thoburn, John 34
Thoburn, Kate Ann Mitchell 5, 6, 7, 10, 12, 17, 108, 111, 124, 131

Thoburn, Lyle 124
Thoburn, Mary 7, 10, 93
Thoburn, Matthew (Thoburn's father) 3
Thoburn, Matthew Martin ("Mattie") 7, 10
Thoburn, Thomas C. 23, 60, 105, 124
Thompson, George W. 101
Tom's Brook, Battle of 107
Tyler, Erastus B. 12, 120
Tynes, Achilles 79

Valley Pike 13, 108
Vaughn, John C. 61
Virginia Central Railroad 33, 45
Virginia Military Institute 47
Virginia units (CSA)
  14th Virginia Cavalry 79
  31st Virginia Infantry 41, 128

Wallace, Lew 61, 83
Wardensville, West Virginia 25, 26
Warren, Gouverneur K. 26
Warrenton, Virginia 12
Washburn, James 68
Washington, D.C. 9, 57, 58, 61, 71, 72, 79, 82, 85, 92, 95, 106, 108, 124, 125
Washington Hall 17
Waterford, Virginia 65
Waynesboro, Virginia 41, 42, 105, 121
Weddle, Jacob 58, 127
Wells, George D. 50, 51, 59, 65, 75, 84, 99, 100, 102, 107, 127, 128
Wellsburg, West Virginia 121, 123
West Virginia units
  1st West Virginia Infantry 1, 3, 8, 9, 11, 12, 13, 14, 17, 18, 21, 26, 28, 29, 35, 41, 58, 61, 119, 120, 121, 122, 123, 127, 128
  4th West Virginia Infantry 50, 61, 96, 127
  10th West Virginia Infantry 84, 101, 133
  11th West Virginia Infantry 68, 101
  12th West Virginia Infantry 21, 28, 29, 61, 76, 114, 127, 128
  15th West Virginia Infantry 68
  Battery D, 1st West Virginia Light Artillery (John Carlin's Battery) 26, 27, 29, 128
Weverton, Maryland 63, 65
Wheeling, West Virginia 1, 4, 5, 7, 8, 11, 17, 35, 38, 58, 110, 111, 116, 125
White Sulphur Springs, West Virginia 53
Wildes, Thomas F. 108
Williamsport, Maryland 59
Wilson, James 110
Wilson, Jeanette (Thoburn) 110
Winchester Pike 72, 99
Winchester, Third Battle of 105

Winchester, Virginia 11, 23, 24, 46, 61, 71, 73, 75, 76, 77, 78, 80, 86, 97, 98, 99, 101, 102, 108, 119, 124
Wolfsville, Maryland 82
Wolftown, Maryland 80
Woodstock, Virginia 25, 26, 27, 35, 36
Wright, Horatio 58, 61, 65, 71, 72, 80

Young, Samuel B.M. 63

About the Author

Scott C. Patchan is a graduate of James Madison University in the Shenandoah Valley. He is the author of many articles and books, including *The Forgotten Fury: The Battle of Piedmont* (1996), *Shenandoah Summer: The 1864 Valley Campaign* (2007), *Second Manassas: Longstreet's Attack and the Struggle for Chinn Ridge* (2011), *The Battle of Piedmont and Hunter's Raid on Staunton* (2011), and *The Last Battle of Winchester: Phil Sheridan, Jubal Early and the 1864 Shenandoah Valley Campaign* (2013).

He has also written feature essays for *Blue and Gray Magazine* on Cool Spring, Rutherford's Farm and Second Kernstown; Third Battle of Winchester, Fisher's Hill, Cedar Creek and two volumes on Second Bull Run. He has also written extensively for *Civil War Magazine*, *North South*, *America's Civil War* and other historical publications.

Scott has twice served as President of Bull Run Civil War Round Table, a member of the Kernstown Battlefield Association's board of directors from 2000-2014, and worked extensively on the interpretation of the Third Winchester battlefield for the Shenandoah Valley Battlefield Foundation. He is also a much sought-after tour guide at both Civil War and Revolutionary War era sites from New York to Georgia.

35th Star Publishing
Charleston, West Virginia
www.35thstar.com

www.ingramcontent.com/pod-product-compliance
Lightning Source LLC
Chambersburg PA
CBHW052204090526
44583CB00015BA/1505